Images of War
With Rommel in the Desert
Tripoli to El Alamein

David Mitchelhill-Green

Pen & Sword
MILITARY

First published in Great Britain in 2017 by
PEN & SWORD MILITARY
an imprint of
Pen & Sword Books Ltd,
47 Church Street,
Barnsley,
South Yorkshire.
S70 2AS

A CIP record for this book is available from the British Library.

ISBN 978 1 47387 875 4

Printed and bound in England
By CPI Group (UK) Ltd, Croydon, CR0 4YY

Pen & Sword Books Ltd incorporates the Imprints of Pen & Sword
Books Archaeology, Atlas, Aviation, Battleground, Discovery, Family
History, History, Maritime, Military, Naval, Politics, Railways, Select,
Transport, True Crime, Fiction, Frontline Books, Leo Cooper,
Praetorian Press, Seaforth Publishing, Wharncliffe and White Owl.

For a complete list of Pen & Sword titles please contact
Pen & Sword Books Limited
47 Church Street, Barnsley, South Yorkshire, S70 2AS, England
E-mail: enquiries@pen-and-sword.co.uk
Website: www.pen-and-sword.co.uk

Contents

Acknowledgments

My sincere appreciation is extended to the following individuals and their collective expertise who helped make this book possible: Bertram Nold, Bob Johnston, Pierce Fox, Markus Wirén, Ilian Filipov, Alex Penner, Greg Singh, James Payne, Fausto Corsetti, and Dr Petra Bopp. Many thanks also to the enthusiastic staff of Pen & Sword: Roni Wilkinson, Matt Jones and Jodie Butterwood.

Notes on Photographic Sources

The majority of photographs used in this book are unpublished snapshots taken by ordinary German and Allied combatants serving in North Africa. At times compromised by poor quality photographic equipment, dust and sand inside cameras, inferior processing and the ravages of time, these images nevertheless depict the life of Rommel's *Afrikaner* with a gritty realism. Supplementing these candid photographs are shots from the US National Archives and Records Administration (NARA).

Abbreviations, Conventions and Definitions

Balkenkreuz	Straight-armed cross symbol of the Wehrmacht
CMP	Canadian Military Pattern
DAK	*Deutsches Afrikakorps* (German Africa Corps)
DAF	British Desert Air Force
Flak	*Flugzeugabwehrkanone* or anti-aircraft gun
Heer	German Army
Jagdgeschwader	Fighter squadron
Kleiner Panzerbefehlswagen	Small command tank
Kraftradfahrer	Motorcyclist
Kriegsmarine	German Navy
Kriegsberichter-Kompanie	War correspondence company
Leichter Funkpanzerwagen	Light radio armoured vehicle
Leichter Panzerspähwagen	Light reconnaissance armoured car
Luftwaffe	German Air Force
OKW	*Oberkommando der Wehrmacht* (the Supreme Armed Forces Command)
Pak	*Panzerabwehrkanone* or anti-tank gun
Panzerkampfwagen	'Armoured fighting vehicle', abbreviated as Pz.Kpfw. or Panzer
Panzerjäger-Abteilung	'Tank hunting battalion'
RAF	Royal Air Force
Reichs-Rundfunk-Gesellschaft	Reich Broadcasting Corporation
Reichspropagandaminister	Minister of propaganda
Schwere Feldhaubitze	Heavy field howitzer
Schwerer Panzerspähwagen	Heavy reconnaissance armored car
Sonderkraftfahrzeug	'Special-purpose vehicle', an ordnance number for military vehicles, abbreviated as 'Sd.Kfz.'

Sperrverband	'Blocking force'
Stabsstaffel	'Staff squadron'
Stuka	*Sturzkampfflugzeug* ('dive bomber')
Vormarsch	'Advance'
Wehrmacht	German Armed Forces
Wehrmacht-Rundfunkempfänger	Wehrmacht broadcast receiver
Zerstörergeschwader	'Destroyer wing'

The term 'British' will be used in its contemporary context, to denote both Empire and Commonwealth troops – who actually outnumbered British personnel for much of the North African Campaign – drawn from the Antipodes, India and South Africa.

Background

The Middle East, a land bridge connecting Europe, Asia and Africa, was the crossroads of the British Empire. The opening of the Suez Canal in 1869 considerably shortened the length of the passage from London to the furthest points of its Empire, which at the time covered a quarter of the earth's landmass, including India, Australia, South Africa, New Zealand, Singapore and Hong Kong. During the First World War, Cairo became the headquarters for British campaigns against Turkey in the Middle East, including the invasion at Gallipoli, and the Western Desert – where motorised warfare first showed its true potential. By 1940, the region was economically, politically and strategically crucial to Britain. The 5 per cent of the world's oil produced there was more than enough to cover Britain's needs, or indeed those of the Axis. It not only shielded India from the Axis, but also provided a buffer against the unknown threat posed by Russia, which had become aligned with Germany under the Russo-German Non-Aggression Pact of August 1939. It also strengthened British prestige. To lose the Middle East, with its oil and strategic significance, would be calamitous for Britain and its allies at a time when it was far from certain whether America would enter the war. Control of the Middle East was, therefore, deemed crucial by Britain's chiefs of staff.

A strategic morass

The signing of the French surrender on 22 June 1940 presented Adolf Hitler with the vexed question: how to overcome Britain? Inside the Führer's headquarters, General Walter Warlimont, deputy chief in the *Oberkommando der Wehrmacht* (OKW), labelled the lack of any clear strategic direction as a 'morass'. A month after the French armistice, in one of the most significant decisions of the war, Hitler directed his army commander in chief, Field Marshal Walther von Brauchitsch, to begin planning for an invasion of the Soviet Union. Germany's strategic die had been cast and all future operations against Britain would be secondary to Hitler's ideological dream of conquering Bolshevik Russia. Yet the problem of crushing Britain remained. Because the Luftwaffe could not achieve the preliminary requirement for an amphibious operation across the English Channel – aerial superiority – Hitler's senior army and naval commanders instead proposed alternative courses of action, including intervention in the Mediterranean and Middle East.

Grand Admiral Erich Raeder, commander in chief of the *Kriegsmarine* (German Navy), urged Hitler to drive the British from the Mediterranean, 'the pivot of their world empire'. He called for the seizure of Gibraltar and the Suez Canal, plus an offensive in Syria and Palestine. In addition to the obvious benefits of such a strategy, Raeder argued that it would forestall the possibility of the British, in concert with the Free French and perhaps the US, from using north-west Africa as a future base from which to attack Italy. Benito Mussolini's impending invasion of Egypt also attracted Berlin's attention. Hitler and Brauchitsch debated sending an armoured detachment to Libya. It was believed that the North African coastal strip would suit mobile warfare, though Italian tanks were deemed inferior to British models. The pair also concluded that an Italian offensive stood little chance of success without German intervention.

To reach Cairo, Mussolini's army would first have to cross the Western Desert, an immense arid region west of the Nile River. Nearly rectangular, the Western Desert stretches 240 miles (390 km) west from the Nile River and, at its widest point, 150 miles (240 km) south from the Mediterranean. A harsh and unforgiving environment for any army, Winston Churchill described to it as an adversary like 'nothing in the world'. Because the desert itself yielded virtually nothing to support an army, every individual item necessary for living and fighting had to be transported from the rear supply bases to the frontlines. A foremost logistical challenge, it was, ironically, compounded by victory – an advancing army gained ground, but its supply lines correspondingly lengthened. It was for this reason that coastal ports such as Tripoli, Tobruk and Benghazi were so valuable.

Determined to wage his own 'private' war, Mussolini, independent of Hitler's victory over Britain, or even his assistance, ordered Marshal Rodolfo Graziani's Tenth Army across the Egyptian frontier on 13 September 1940. The invasion – astonishingly – lacked any actual territorial objectives. (Mussolini had earlier declared war against Britain on 10 June with optimistic plans to 'dominate the Mediterranean at the earliest possible moment'.) As British intelligence in Cairo correctly predicted, the Italian 'colonial offensive' advanced a mere 65 miles before halting at Sidi Barrani, some 80 miles short of the British base at Mersa Matruh. While the Italian propaganda machine worked tirelessly to publicise the 'conquest', the encamped army commenced construction of a series of fortified camps – positions resembling the 'boxes' that the

British would later construct along the Gazala Line to the west of Tobruk in 1942.

In early October 1940, General Franz Halder, chief of staff of OKH, noted in his diary how the Italians, in the absence of 'any conclusive success', were showing renewed interest in receiving German assistance. 'They want one armoured division; transfer would take ten weeks, and it would be the New Year before the division could go into action.' As the possibility of Wehrmacht involvement in North Africa developed, a delegation under General Ritta von Thoma travelled to Libya to assess the battlefield first-hand. (Colonel Baron Geyr von Schweppenburg, the German military attaché in London, had already inspected the British garrison in Egypt and the natural obstacle of the Western Desert in 1937. In his opinion, 'any [Axis] offensive from the west must come to a halt on the Nile if not before.') Von Thoma's report was critical of Graziani and the slow progress of Italians preparations to capture Mersa Matruh. It even advised that the African theatre was suitable only for the type of guerrilla warfare Colonel Paul von Lettow-Vorbeck had waged during the First World War in East Africa. Potential Axis collaboration received a further setback when Mussolini dispatched a letter to Berlin on 23 October snubbing German aid across the Mediterranean and North Africa. In line with his sequestered ambitions, the Duce also argued Italy's case for invading Greece, a fiasco he launched five days later.

Rome's stubbornness continued amid the disastrous campaign in Greece. In mid-November Marshal Pietro Badoglio, Italian chief of staff, informed Field Marshal Wilhelm Keitel, chief of OKW, that German tanks would be 'ineffective' and unable to operate in the sandy desert environment! Despite Italy's on-going aversion to receiving much-needed modern armoured reinforcements, Berlin continued to examine transporting armour and troops to North Africa, as well as intervening in Greece. But as Hitler complained: 'The lunacy about it all is that on the one hand the Italians are screaming blue murder and painting their shortages of arms and equipment in the blackest terms, and on the other hand they are so jealous and infantile that they find the using of using German soldiers and German materials quite repugnant.' Frustrated by his ally's indecision and hesitancy, Halder's diary entry on 5 December reads: 'Libya: no longer contemplated.'

Italian obstinacy regarding German ground forces, however, quickly vanished after Britain's (victorious) first offensive in the Western Desert, Operation Compass, began on 9 December 1940. A request by Badoglio's successor, Marshal Ugo Cavallero, on December 18 for a Panzer division, plus an urgent appeal by Mussolini, persuaded

Hitler to formally commit troops to Africa. During a meeting at his Bavarian alpine retreat, the Berghof, on 8-9 January 1941 he announced that a *Sperrverband* (blocking force) would be sent to Libya on 22 February. The Wehrmacht's involvement in North Africa was sanctioned in Hitler's Directive No. 22, dated 11 January 1941:

'German Support for battles in the Mediterranean area

The situation in the Mediterranean area, where England is employing superior forces against our allies, requires that German should assist for reasons of strategy, politics, and psychology. Tripolitania must be held …'

Hitler met with Mussolini a week later to authorise Operation *Sonnenblume* (Sunflower), an ultimately fateful entanglement. In light of his forthcoming invasion of the Soviet Union, Hitler intended to commit just enough troops to bolster the defence of Tripoli. According to former General Siegfried Westphal, the undertaking was designed 'to tie down as many British troops as possible and to cover the southern flank of Europe. We had never had the intention of conquering Egypt or crossing the Suez Canal.' The first Axis units to be shipped across the Mediterranean included the German 5th Light Division, plus the Italian 'Ariete' Armoured and 'Trento' Motorised Infantry Divisions. The commanding officer of the German expeditionary force, the *Deutsches Afrikakorps* (DAK), was announced on 3 February 1941: *Generalleutnant* Erwin Rommel.

The Western Desert Campaign

The war across Libya and Egypt was characterised by a pendulum-like series of advances and withdrawals across tracts of mostly worthless desert between long periods of inactivity. It began with Graziani's abortive march on Cairo in September 1940. General Archibald Wavell's counter-offensive, Operation Compass (lead by General Richard O'Connor), quickly retook Sidi Barrani, smashing the Italian threat to Egypt. Pressing west, O'Connor's Western Desert Force captured the Italian coastal fortresses at Bardia and Tobruk before utterly destroying the Italian Tenth Army. A march on Tripoli, which may have removed the Axis from North Africa two years before eventual defeat in Tunisia in 1942, was prevented by Whitehall's decision to intervene in Greece.

No sooner had Rommel arrived in Tripoli on 12 February 1941 than he was airborne on a reconnaissance flight scouting the unknown desert terrain. While British intelligence incorrectly concluded that the no immediate danger of an Axis offensive existed, Rommel was planning to ignore his own directives and reverse the British tide in North Africa. German troops first made contact with a British patrol in a brief skirmish near El Agheila on 24 February. Urging his men forward across the desert, often short of fuel and ammunition, Rommel hoped to deceive his enemy as to his true strength. The mixed British garrison that retreated into Tobruk withstood a series of attacks in mid-April and earlier May, forcing Rommel to besiege the fortress, a barb on his flank constraining his forward units from pressing deep into Egypt.

After two abortive counter-offensives (Brevity and Battleaxe), General Claude Auchinleck's Operation Crusader finally relieved Tobruk in December 1941 after a 242-day siege. Axis forces fell back to El Agheila. Once again British forces were prevented from pushing onward to Tripoli, this time by Japan's entry into the war and the need to transfer men and equipment to the Far East. The see-sawing campaign placed additional strain on the British Eighth Army as its tenuous communication and supply lines lengthened. Rommel, in contrast, was now much closer to his own points of supply; 'the battle is fought and decided by the quartermasters before the shooting begins,' he would later reflect.

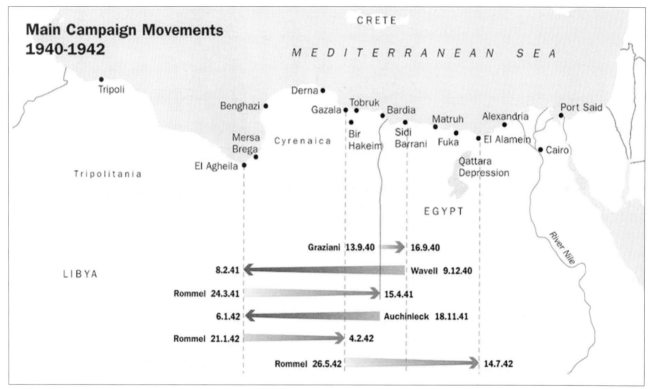

Main Campaign Movements 1940-1942

CRETE

MEDITERRANEAN SEA

Tripoli

Derna

Benghazi
Gazala
Tobruk
Bardia
Matruh
Alexandria
Port Said

Mersa Brega
Cyrenaica
Bir Hakeim
Sidi Barrani
Fuka
El Alamein

El Agheila
Qattara Depression
Cairo

Tripolitania

EGYPT

River Nile

LIBYA

Graziani 13.9.40 → 16.9.40

8.2.41 ← Wavell 9.12.40

Rommel 24.3.41 → 15.4.41

6.1.42 ← Auchinleck 18.11.41

Rommel 21.1.42 → 4.2.42

Rommel 26.5.42 → 14.7.42

The ebb and flow of the North African Campaign across Libya and Egypt, 1940-1942.

A replenished Rommel launched a new offensive on 21 January 1942. Once again the British were caught off-guard, the success of the *Panzerarmee* Afrika surprising both OKW and the British. Churchill prodded Auchinleck to resume the offensive during a pause in the fighting, but once again, Rommel pre-empted his opponent. On 26 May, in the midst of a sandstorm, he steered his panzers toward the southern end of Auchlinleck's Gazala defences while the Italians launched a frontal assault in the north. Overwhelming the Free French defenders at Bir Hacheim, Rommel reached Tobruk on 19 June. The Axis assault the following day overwhelmed the ad-hoc British force, which surrendered twenty hours later. Rommel's greatest victory, as General Franz Halder noted, was 'of equally great value from the military and the political aspect'. In gratitude, Hitler immediately promoted 49-year-old Rommel to field marshal, Germany's youngest.

Sensitive to the menace posed by the Rommel 'phenomenon', Auchinleck urged his officers not to be taken in by the cult of personality that had grown around their audacious adversary: 'There exists a very real danger that our friend Rommel is becoming a kind of magician or bogey-man to our troops.'

Hitler approved Rommel's ambitious proposal to chase the retreating British forces into Egypt. This was, Rommel wrote in retrospect, 'the one moment in the African war when the road to Alexandria lay open and virtually undefended.' Cancelling orders for rest days, he harried the *Panzerarmee* to move off again. Mersa Matruh fell on 29 June. Rommel's vanguard reached El Alamein in early July – the apex of his African adventure.

Chapter 1
German Intervention in North Africa

Britain's naval bases at Gibraltar and Egypt had long rankled the Italians as maritime manacles 'imprisoning' them within the confines of the Mediterranean. Rome yearned for the ancient ideal – *mare nostrum* (our sea) – rather than an 'Italian lake' constricted by small British-controlled outlets at either end. Thus, in order to gain 'free access to the oceans', Mussolini planned to conquer Egypt – part of a grander vision for a new Roman Empire stretching from the Mediterranean to the Indian Ocean. Foreshadowing his expansion across the Middle East, during a visit to Libya in March 1937 Mussolini declared himself the 'Protector of Islam'. For many Arabs, however, Italy merely represented another hungry imperialist power rather than a path to independence.

During his March 1937 visit to Libya, an Italian colony since 1911, Mussolini inaugurated a new coastal road: the *Litoranea Balbo*, later dubbed the *Via Balbia*, which stretched some 1,300 miles (2,090km) between the Tunisia and Egyptian frontiers.

The strategic carriageway was vital for the growth of his North African colony and the future movement of troops in times of war.

Marshal Rodolfo Graziani's invasion of Egypt on 13 September 1940 paused after three days, having advanced a mere 65 miles across worthless desert to Sidi Barrani, some 300 miles (480km) short of Cairo. Lieutenant-General Richard O'Connor's counter-offensive, Operation Compass, was launched three months later on 9 December 1940. Unfolding into a brilliant campaign that decimated the Italian Tenth Army, O'Connor advanced 650 miles (1,050km) and captured 130,000 Italian troops. 'I think this may be termed a complete victory as none of the enemy escaped,' he later noted. Yet the opportunity to push on to Tripoli and rout the Italian threat slipped through Britain's fingers as Churchill withdrew forces to fight the Germans in Greece. O'Connor later blamed himself, declaring that 'it was quite inexcusable'.

Wehrmacht materiel bound for Libya was transported by train through the Brenner Pass to southern Italian ports for passage across the Mediterranean to Tripoli. Inter-service conflict arose over the transport of vehicles and men – Germany's *Heer* (army) wanted to jointly load vessels together to ensure units were ready to move out upon disembarkation; the *Kriegsmarine* argued that more men would be lost if slower vessels carrying vehicles were sunk. As it eventuated, vehicles and equipment were separated after the loss of several transports.

Loading a Mittlerer Zugkraftwagen 8-ton (Sd. Kfz. 7) halftrack. Although fully motorised, the first German vehicles rushed to Africa were designed to operate under European conditions. Lacking the appropriate air filters and lubricants, many vehicles succumbed to the brutal desert conditions. Due to their hasty departure, the first vehicles unloaded in Tripoli retained their Dunkelgrau RAL 7021 colour scheme. Curiously, a British intelligence report later noted German tanks 'painted black, evidently to aid their anti-tank gunners in quick daytime identifications while also serving as night camouflage'.

En route to Africa aboard a fast passenger liner. Note the Spica class torpedo boats at anchor. Of the thirty vessels of this class built for the *Regia Marina* (Royal [Italian] Navy), twenty-three were lost in the war. Despite a chronic fuel oil shortage, the *Regia Marina* made a substantial contribution to the maintenance of Rommel's maritime supply lines.

Pensive passengers. The Mediterranean crossing grew increasingly hazardous for Axis convoys ferrying troops and materiel to Libya. Two Italian liners turned troopships (MS *Oceania* and *Neptunia*), for example, were sunk in a heavily armed convoy by the British submarine *Upholder* on 18 September 1941, some 60 miles (97km) off Tripoli. British submarines sunk forty-nine Axis troop/supply ships in the period from June to September 1941 alone.

On the lookout for enemy aircraft with *Maschinengewehr* 34, or MG 34 machine gun on a tripod anti-aircraft mount. British aircraft and submarines operating out of Malta Axis convoys took an increasing toll. Whereas 16 per cent of Axis cargo was lost between June to October 1941, in November 1941 this figure jumped to 62 per cent, further compounding Rommel's chronic supply shortage. Plans for an Axis invasion of Malta, dubbed Operation Hercules, were abandoned after Rommel's 1942 conquest of Tobruk.

Siegfried Westphal: 'Unloading in the harbour at Tripoli was continuous throughout the sunny days of February, not only by day, but also, despite the danger of air attack, by the light of searchlights at night.'

A Sd.Kfz. 265 *kleiner Panzerbefehlswagen* from the 5th Panzer Regiment, 5th Light Division, is lowered onto the Tripoli docks in March 1941. Note the symbol of the 3rd Panzer Division still visible on the superstructure.

Leutnant Joachim Schorm's (5th Panzer Regiment) diary entry for 12 March 1941: '1400 hours. We move to the town and take up our position in the parade … At 1800 hours, the panzers rumble through the port along the *Via Balbia* towards the east. All night long we are greeted by soldiers, settlers and natives …'

A *Leichter Panzerspähwagen* (2cm) Sd.Kfz.222 armoured car parading through Tripoli. A total of 989 of these reconnaissance vehicles were produced from 1936 to June 1943. *Propagandakompanie* camera in the background.

Chapter 2
Tourists in Uniform

'In Africa there awaited the great adventure'
--Leutnant Ralph Ringer, 104 Panzer Grenadier Regiment

The Second World War was a defining moment in photography. Never before had the experience of war been so readily captured on film. Nazi Germany viewed the camera as a powerful propaganda weapon with millions of images taken by both official and amateur photographers. In 1933, *Reichspropagandaminister* Joseph Goebbels urged 'every German' to possess a camera. He later implored the 'army of millions of amateur photographers' to individually enlighten the nation; the 'experience of the individual has become a peoples' experience' he declared. The *Reichsministerium für Volksaufklärung und Propaganda* (Reich Ministry for Popular Enlightenment and Propaganda) later urged the 10 per cent of Germans – approximately seven million people – who owned a camera in 1939 to continue their craft in wartime. Capturing war in 'fine detail' was easily achievable through a range of lightweight precision cameras that offered a range of features, including a viewfinder, anastigmatic lenses and a variable shutter speed.

The unworldly lava flows of Mount Vesuvius, outside Naples, were a common attraction for troops en route to Libya. The volcano's last major eruption occurred during the Italian Campaign in March 1944.

A visit to the Parthenon in Athens. Note the swastika flying at the Belvedere to the left of the ancient citadel. The Nazi flag was first raised at the eastern end at the Acropolis on 27 April 1941, exactly three weeks after the German invasion. Greece was jointly occupied by Germany, Bulgaria and Italy, with German forces responsible for the occupation of Athens until its liberation in

Snapshots were routinely exchanged or purchased to create a personal military service record. This commonly found photo in wartime albums shows Rommel enjoying a toast with the officers of an Italian submarine, possibly the Foca Class *Atropo*, during a visit to Bardia. Italian submarines were used as early as April 1941 to transport fuel and ammunition for the most advanced elements of the *Afrikakorps*. Forty-six such supply missions were undertaken in the second half of 1941.

Distant snapshots of the 'Desert Fox'. Rommel was easily the most photographed individual in North Africa.

'The Magic of the Orient'

'The number of volunteers for this theatre of war was understandably large, as the magic of the Orient has always attracted youth,' retired General Siegfried Westphal reminisced after the war. 'There were dreams of adventures, of lion hunts, of rides on camels with the speed of an arrow, of brilliantly attractive dancing girls in refreshing oases.' The diary entry of a Leutnant in the 104th Panzer Grenadier Regiment, 21st Panzer Division, in July 1942 provides an insight into the attraction Africa held: 'We are all twenty-one years old and crazy. Crazy because we have volunteered of our own free will to go to Africa and have talked about nothing else for weeks and haven't been able to think about anything else either. Fantasy has had a free rein – Africa – that's tropical nights, palm trees, sea breezes, natives, oases and tropical helmets. Also a little war, but how can we be anything but victorious? Rommel had taken Tobruk a few days previously so how long would it be before we were in Cairo, Alexandria and at the Suez Canal? Cairo, and we would be in white tropical uniforms. Previously the doings of the Afrikakorps had been featured in the newspapers – by God how we would enjoy that! Out in Africa we wouldn't be one of the crowd and would make a name for ourselves. Day and night we built castles in the air, only to get away from here, away from this morass, a meandering army and the training of recruits. Most of us had already "enjoyed" Russia and had no desire to return to the dirt, the cold and Ivan … Like madmen we jumped around and hugged each other, we really were going to Africa!' Another veteran of the *Ostfront*, Hans von luck, mused: 'What would await us? We were highly expectant, almost eager for adventure.'

A young member of the 104th Panzer Grenadier Regiment recounted his flight from Brindisi to Africa on 22 April 1942: '… early one morning, we were taken to the aerodrome, now this was it. The many Ju 52s that would fly us to Africa made an impressive sight – there must have been about thirty-five in all. We were divided into groups of eighteen and we were taken to the plane, life jackets were handed out and then we had to get in. I had a window seat so I could easily see what went on. Who would have thought nine months ago, whilst training as radio operators in Brunswick, that we would be flying today to Africa. The machines taxied to the runway and off we went towards Africa, for all of us it was a fantastic sight to see all the machines in the air.'

Africa's exotic allure featured heavily in German propaganda and soldier's snapshots. Imperialist Germany acquired four African colonies during the late nineteenth century: German Southwest Africa (Namibia), German East Africa (now part of Tanzania), Togo and Cameroon. All were subsequently ceded to the victors of 1918 under the Treaty of Versailles. From an economic perspective, Hitler called for the return of the colonies in a 1937 speech: 'our demand for colonies for our densely populated country will be put forward again and again.' While various colonial organisations in the Third Reich proposed the recovery of these former possessions, Hitler vacillated. 'The day we have firmly organised Europe we shall be able to look out towards Africa…' he stated on 22 February 1942. Already mired on the Eastern Front, such aspirations were soon abandoned with the Wehrmacht embroiled in the Battle for Stalingrad.

Die Wehrmacht, 4 June 1941: '…a talisman to a combatant of our *Afrikakorps*'. Chameleons were seen as the bearers of good news from the gods, especially for immortality and healing, in African mythology.

A meeting of cultures. Hans-Joachim Schraepler described an incident when Hauptmann Hermann Aldinger, Rommel's aide, attempted to photograph an Arab woman: 'Although he approached her as if he was stalking a deer, it was impossible. The woman ran away, left her oxen at the well and was not seen again. Arabs came running, demanding cigarettes.'

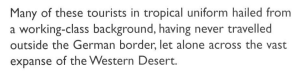

Many of these tourists in tropical uniform hailed from a working-class background, having never travelled outside the German border, let alone across the vast expanse of the Western Desert.

A world away from continental Europe. Images of German solders posing with Libyan natives were commonplace in wartime photo albums. A personal letter found on a captured German soldier in May 1941 highlights the feeling towards the men serving in Africa: '…there is nothing better I can do than congratulate you from the bottom of my heart for having reached your destination so soon and for being in such a wonderful theatre of war. I can well imagine that a high degree of physical endurance is required where you are, than, for example, here in France, but I am sure that this will be to your liking…you will have to endure everything; burning heat, tortures of thirst, the biting cold of the night, long marches and stormy conflicts. One might almost envy you [and] all these hardships…'

Palm trees naturally featured in many soldiers' albums and, on this occasion, as the butt of Australian humour. A stylised palm tree with superimposed swastika became the iconic symbol of the *Deutsches Afrikakorps* on 1 April 1941.

Photographs of mosques and
camels became popular
photographic motifs.

Compared to their comrades in Europe, German soldiers serving in Africa received an 'overseas allowance' of 2 *Reichsmarks* a day for enlisted personnel, 3 *Reichsmarks* a day for non-commissioned officers and 4 *Reichsmarks* for officers.

Afrikakorps and Luftwaffe personnel pose for portraits beside indigenous modes of desert transport.

Bazaars and street vendors were popular attractions. Training films for troops bound for Africa warned of the dangers of food poisoning and intestinal infections from contaminated water.

The ancient Greek and Roman ruins of Sabratha, Leptis Magna and Cyrene were also popular 'tourist' sites. Over the millennia, the Phoenicians, Greeks, Ptolemies, Romans, Arabs and Ottoman Turks ruled the area we know today as Libya – a name bestowed by Italy on its North African colony in 1934. From 1943 to 1951 the country was under Allied occupation. Italy formally relinquished all claims to Libya in 1947.

15 May 1941. Rommel is shown around the ruins of Cyrene by *Generale d'Armata* Italo Gariboldi. The former's adjutant wrote home how 'some have whispered mockingly that Rommel would have preferred to see the ruins of which he himself was responsible ...'

'Through the desert sand, hot and sunburned, men are going on a major hunt with loud fanfares of the hallali. 'We are the hunters in a large game reserve: the German Army in Africa, Hurray! Hurray! Safari!' Lyrics to the first verse of the DAK song *Heia Safari*.

The lure of the Orient, however, soon faded. 'Disappointment was naturally inevitable', Westphal observed, 'and was often extremely great. The campaign in Africa very quickly became popular with the German people, probably in particular owing to the chivalrous conduct of the Desert War. This is very remarkable, as the minds of the overwhelming majority of the people of our country had a continental bias. It was an uncanny feeling for our soldiers to know that the Mediterranean lay between them and their home country. They suffered from this, and in many cases experienced severe attacks of homesickness. This continental attitude of mind to which I have just referred displayed itself in another very curious manner; there were high-ranking military persons who regarded our "unauthorised absence" from the Eastern campaign. They failed to understand the meaning of our dispatch to the Libyan desert.'

Chapter 3
Wüste (Desert)

Of the Libyan desert, 'here, for the first time', *Generalmajor* Alfred Toppe wrote in his post-war report, 'the units had to cross a long stretch of desert, some units for 186 miles (300km) and more, and while doing so, they had to gather the experience they lacked. This experience included recognition of the necessity to carry along ample supplies of fuel and water and the difficulties of orientation … The available maps, which were reprints of Italian maps, were inadequate. Practically no reference points existed so that all orientation had to be done by compass. Furthermore, the eyes of the troops had to become accustomed to the glare of the sun, which made contours unclear. Thus, it was extremely difficult to recognise objects – for instance, to differentiate between tanks and trucks.'

Toppe: 'At first, several instances occurred where severe losses were suffered owing to the bunching up of vehicles and troops. It was weeks before the troops learned to counter this new combat factor by a wide dispersal of units in breadth and depth – a particularly important requirement in the desert, where no cover whatever is to be found. (The minimum distance between vehicles should be 50 and if possible 100 meters.) It also proved necessary to dig in immediately all vehicles that were halted for any considerable time. They were to be dug into the ground to at least a depth that protected the axles in order to lessen the effects of bomb fragments. In the same measure, it was also necessary to camouflage the vehicles. This was only possible with the use of camouflage nets so that it was extremely difficult. Furthermore, it was now necessary for each and every man to dig a foxhole as protection during air raids.'

Leutnant Joachim Schorm, 5th Panzer Regiment, observed how the 'war in Africa is quite different from the war in Europe. That is to say, it is absolutely individual. Here there are not the masses of men and material. Nobody and nothing can be concealed.' The desert was an unfamiliar hostile environment for the *Afrikakorps*, unlike the Italians and British, both of whom were familiar with the bleak wilderness. Note the symbol of the 21st Panzer Division on the door above the DAK emblem.

Exposed and visible. Rocks are piled to protect the front tyres from the sun and the windscreen in this Auto Union/Horch 901 Type 40 is covered to prevent reflections.

Troops in the front lines lacked shelter and spent the night in their position or underneath, or beside, their vehicle.

Shadows in the open desert expanse exaggerated the size of objects, making it mandatory for troops to dig themselves in. 'The troops in Africa', Toppe explained, were used to doing so as soon as they had reached their destination, if only from the wish to survive.'

The romantic ideal of desert warfare is one of armies sallying forth untethered. Rather than an arena of total freedom, however, operations in the desert were reliant upon lengthy and vulnerable supply lines. The sinking of a supply convoy, or the delay of a motorised column carrying fuel or ammunition, could halt all movement. Likewise, mechanical breakdowns, poor weather, difficult terrain or aerial attack could encumber mobility – the essence of German warfare.

Tell-tale tracks left by armoured vehicles were eventually eroded by shifting sand or by wheeled vehicles running over them. It was also possible to deceive the enemy by running tracks away from the intended direction of attack, a feint out of all proportion to the effort involved.

The *Via Balbia* had a lot to answer for, an *Afrikakorps* veteran mused: 'If it had never been built, there would have been no war in Africa.' The Germans soon discovered that fuel consumption on the sealed road was no higher than in Europe. Desert marches, however, were another matter with wheeled vehicles on average using 50 per cent more fuel, full or half-tracked vehicles an extra 30 per cent. Oil changes were more frequent than in Europe, at least every 625 miles (1,000km). In a letter home in April 1941, Hans-Joachim Schraepler outlined his concerns regarding fuel and transport shortages: 'I am very much concerned whether we have enough vehicles … the equipment of the corps staff is bad. The gentlemen in Berlin, having no notion of Africa and its local conditions, make financial savings in the wrong places. It will have consequences … supply of water and fuel is difficult. I hope we can keep up the current pace …'

Libya is divided into two territories: Cyrenaica in the east and Tripolitania in the west (although the Germans and Italians referred to western Libya as Cyrenaica and the area east of Gazala as Marmarica). The Arco dei Fileni, marking the frontier between Cyrenaica and Tripolitania, was unveiled before Mussolini on 16 March 1937. The colossal arch featured in many soldiers' photographs as a prominent landmark against the largely featureless desert. A fixture in the tide of war: German troops referred to it as *'Arco vor und zurück'* – the 'To and fro Arch', the British 'Marble Arch'.

The Via Balbia, wrote Rommel, stretched like a black band through 'desolate country, in which no tree or shrub was visible as far as the eye could reach.' Note the overturned vehicle, a casualty of the narrow ribbon of asphalt soon to be riddled with potholes and bomb craters.

Armour plating baked in the midday sun. Images from a propaganda newsreel show soldiers frying an egg on the scorching armour plate of their Pz.Kpfw. II. 'The heat during the day gradually became unbearable', Hans von Luck recalled. 'Some men really did fry eggs on the overheated armour plating of the tanks. It was no fairy tale; I have done it myself.' But as *Oberleutnant* Harald Kuhn, 5th Panzer Regiment, wrote, 'Even if that event were possible, where were we supposed to get the eggs and, moreover, the grease?'

June to August was the hottest time of the year with midday temperatures occasionally soaring past 50°C (122°F). Daily variations could be extreme with temperatures plummeting at night to near freezing.

A natural enemy. 'It was a wretched business', wrote Max Reisch, 'fighting the desert, the heat, the floods, other human beings, not to mention your own frayed nerves'

Storms during the winter months would occasionally flood the desert. Wadis (a usually dry depression or riverbed) would rapidly fill with flash floods sweeping away men and equipment unfortunate enough to be caught in the path of the torrent. Hans von Luck recalled one occasion in which a truck hauling a field kitchen was swept hundreds of metres along a wadi by a fast moving wave. Toppe observed that 'in spite of the fact that the troops had been warned and were required to evacuate the wadis, there were still numerous living quarters in the valleys during the first big rainfall. The water began to rise during the night and washed away tents and motor vehicles.'

The desert awash with flowers after rain. A DAK interpreter wrote of the sudden change that spring brought: 'I have never seen colours like these: the desert is a coast-to-coast carpet of vivid reds, lemon yellows, purples, lilacs, greens, oranges, violets and white.'

The desert, as these great-coated soldiers experienced, could be bitterly cold. 'Warm clothing after sundown was particularly important in the desert,' Toppe noted, 'and especially so for new arrivals, as a precaution against dysentery and skin diseases, since the difference between the daytime temperatures and those at night was extreme. After sunset, it was absolutely essential for every man to wear trousers and [woollen] bellybands. Experience showed, in fact, that it was advisable to wear the latter day and night.'

The cold, wrote one soldier, left him frozen like a 'naked ski instructor', it 'pierces right through everything in the constant wind. One's feet aren't warm until midday.'

In addition to the extremes of temperature and rainfall, the troops in the desert endured blinding sandstorms caused by fierce winds from the Sahara carrying fine particles of sand, a phenomenon known to Italians as a *ghibli* and the British as a *khamsin*. Von Luck recalled that such storms usually lasted one day, but could be as long as three. 'One could see it coming. The sky grew dark, the fine sand penetrated every pore and made any movement, let alone any military operation, impossible.'

For the men on the ground, the sandstorms were a curse. Visibility was reduced to barely a few yards; vehicle maintenance would cease while weapons clogged with fine dust and lungs choked. Under Bedouin law, it was even permissible for a man to be found innocent of killing his wife should a *khamsin* last five days! Compounding the adversity of desert warfare, many men battled depression. As an Italian soldier wrote in 1940: 'The sand seems always to be in our mouths, in our hair and our clothes, and it is impossible to get cool. Only troops of the highest morale and courage would endure privations like these.' An Italian major in a Combat Sappers Battalion took advantage of a *ghibli* to pen a letter to his wife: 'All the dust from the tracks, ground to a fine powder by the streams of tanks and trucks, has risen up in one dense uniform cloud; you can't see ten yards ahead of you. A day therefore of unexpected, if not exactly comfortable, tranquillity, which I will turn to good use by sending you something better than the usual brief postcard...' On the other side, an article in *Life* magazine on 20 July 1942 disingenuously claimed that the men of the *Afrikakorps* were 'meticulously trained to long hours in tanks, to long runs without water, to sand in their food and hair and bedding, to fly bites and sores, to a beating, unending wind sandpapering their faces...'

A Volkswagen Type 82, known as a *Kübelwagen*, at speed leaves a wake of dust – 'a betrayer', noted Toppe, 'that enables observers, both from the ground and the air, to perceive every movement for great distances, even by individual vehicles.'

'The generation of dust', reported Toppe, 'made it practically impossible to conceal marching columns. Dust clouds could be seen even at great distances and enabled one to recognise the size of the columns and sometimes even the type of vehicles (wheeled or tracklaying).'

Field maintenance on a Ford G 917 T. The amount of water needed for vehicle radiators varied according to the type of engine, fluctuating between 3 and 10 litres a day. The figures for the water rations were generally the same at all times of the year.

Uneven terrain presented yet another threat for the suspension wheeled vehicles designed for European conditions. Major Ernst-Otto Ballerstedt, 115th Motorised Infantry Regiment, advised that drivers should be accustomed to direction finding in the open without reference points, driving without lights, having a 'quick perception' of sudden obstacles such as large potholes and accurately assessing the ground clearance of a vehicle.

A chronic shortage of vehicles saw captured enemy vehicles readily pressed into service, in this instance an ex-Australian vehicle: 'Ambulance, Indian Army Type (Aust.), No. 1'.

Resting beside a Faun type L 354. The DAK faced enormous supply challenges. 'Even when our supplies did reach Africa', *Generalmajor* Friedrich von Mellenthin explained, 'it was no easy matter to move them to the front, because of the great distances involved … When we were at Alamein, many of our supplies had to be hauled 1,400 miles [2,250km] from Tripoli.'

Luftwaffe Mercedes Benz type 170 V, one of 72,000 examples manufactured from 1935 to 1942.

A report issued by the *Panzertruppenschule* II (Armoured Troops School No.2) at Wünsdorf (16 October 1941), 'Lessons from the African Theatre of War', concluded that ordinary cars were 'unsatisfactory in the desert'. As one officer bemoaned five months earlier, 'I currently have no cars to give. Total losses are on the agenda. The best cars don't stand long journeys on this difficult terrain.'

The *Panzertruppenschule* report found that the 'light cross-country car' (VW Type 82 Kübelwagen) can get through any terrain except shifting sand dunes.' Replacing the regular 5.25-16 tyres with larger 22-67 sand tyres required moving the vehicle's front axle.

The same report noted that 'medium and heavy cross-country cars can cross any type of country.' Nevertheless, their spring suspension systems needed special attention. The spiral springs used in the Type 16 and 17 command cars did not prove practical in desert terrain, breaking easily and causing a supply bottleneck. Leaf springs were judged stronger and more suitable.

With regard to heavier transport, it was discovered that 'Ford V8 (above) and Opel Blitz "S" (left) trucks do not stand up well on long desert drives, but show few complete breakdowns. Twin wheels have been found to be unsatisfactory, as stones get jammed between them.'

Major Ernst-Otto Ballerstedt noted, in August 1941, that German motor transport (MT) had proven to be 'only partially satisfactory. The maximum loads laid down for European roads and country conditions are too high for the desert. A 3.5-ton truck is heavily overloaded with a 3.5-ton load in desert country. For this reason, the establishment of MT must be increased, particularly for heavy weapons.' A shortage of vehicles would lead to 'immediate unbearable hardship, threatening not only the fighting efficiency but even the existence of the troops'.

The *Panzertruppenschule* report also documented how the 'only vehicle which has mastered all types of cross-country going is the half-track carrier. It can surmount dunes of shifting sand with a 40 percent gradient, without difficulty or help.' The half-track is a Sd.Kfz. 251.

Pz.Kpfw. IIIs spaced out during a march along the Via Balbia – the road to Cairo – with an early *mittlerer geländegängiger Personenkraftwagen* (medium cross-country passenger car) Auto Union/Horch 901 in the foreground.

Camouflage, Toppe noted, 'is very difficult in the desert and, in many cases, impossible … nevertheless, troop concentrations can be camouflaged, if great care is used. Depressions in the terrain will have to be exploited for this purpose. All vehicles will have to be covered with camouflage nets and vegetation (camel's thorn) attached to the nets.'

Camel thorn bush used to camouflage a Pz.Kpfw. IV. Caution was needed since carelessly removing branches, camel thorn or grass clumps immediately around a vehicle could render it even more prominent against a bare, denuded background.

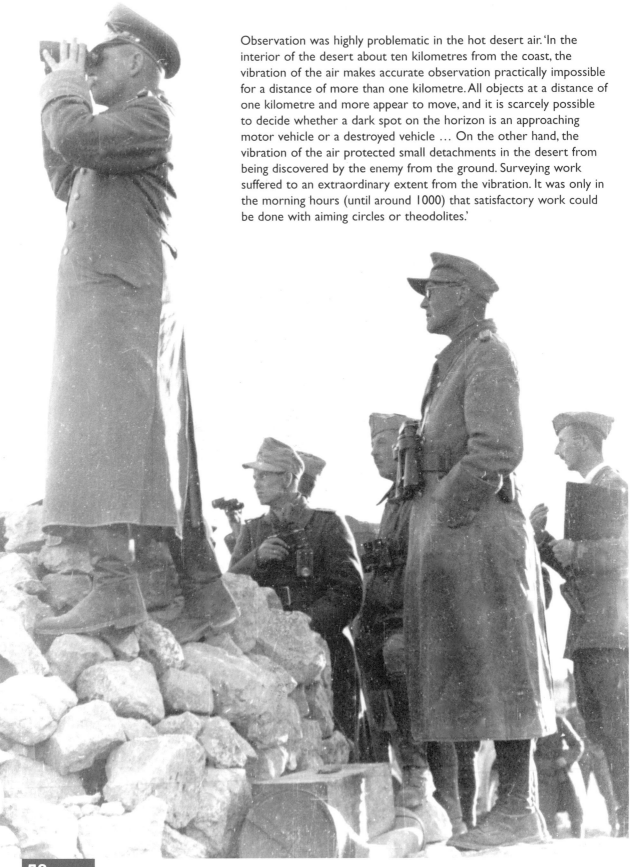

Observation was highly problematic in the hot desert air. 'In the interior of the desert about ten kilometres from the coast, the vibration of the air makes accurate observation practically impossible for a distance of more than one kilometre. All objects at a distance of one kilometre and more appear to move, and it is scarcely possible to decide whether a dark spot on the horizon is an approaching motor vehicle or a destroyed vehicle ... On the other hand, the vibration of the air protected small detachments in the desert from being discovered by the enemy from the ground. Surveying work suffered to an extraordinary extent from the vibration. It was only in the morning hours (until around 1000) that satisfactory work could be done with aiming circles or theodolites.'

Delivering water to the line via the ubiquitous *Wehrmacht Einheitskanister*, the robust steel 20-litre container was submitted by Vinzenz Grünvogel for a 1936 Wehrmacht tender. The well-engineered container was vastly superior to the British fuel equivalent, or 'flimsy' as it was derided, and the standard 55-gallon fuel drum used by the US Army. Both British and American forces copied the 'Jerry can', as it was dubbed.

Rommel's adjutant noted on 20 May 1941 that each man drinks 'several litres' of water each day. *Leutnant* Rudolf Wendorff, 5th Panzer Regiment, described the quality and availability of water: 'Located between the Mediterranean and the so-called coastal road, there was no normal water; instead there were a few wells with water that had salt in it, which we had to get used to … Once a week, we receive normal salt-free water for our tea and for us personally. That was a day of celebration …'

A German Ford tows an Italian 5,000 litre tank, built by Viberti on a standard medium trailer (*rimorchio unificato medio*).

A seasoned *Afrikaner* imbibes directly from a *Wehrmacht-Einheitskanister,* the white cross denoting water. Recalling his time in the desert, Hans von Luck wrote of a daily routine, drinking a litre of water in the morning, nothing thoughout the day, then a 'second half' in the evening. Regulations similarly called for water never to be drunk during the day.

Large amounts of water were also found in coastal wells, known as a 'Bir' in Arabic, and in the chains of oases extending along the nineteenth parallel, including the Siwa, Giarabub, Gialo and Marada.

Wrote one German officer: '… one drinks three times as much as in Germany. Hence, the body has to adapt itself a lot. But we manage. Where would you find anybody in Germany who would drink water of this colour and taste? It looks like cocoa and tastes of sulphur. But that is good for us, as otherwise it would stimulate one's thirst …'

Alighting from a Krupp L2 H143, Rommel inspects a desert well. Both sides accused the other of tainting previous wells with oil, though some believed that it had been a natural phenomenon arising from underground oil reserves.

'Excretory matter', Toppe cautioned, 'should be buried after each movement of the bowels (the "spade system" is preferable to the latrine system).' Similarly, all refuse had to be buried immediately to prevent the spread of infection. But as one British desert veteran wrote, there was additional hardship for the *Afrikakorps*: 'Its units were close to and sometimes intermingled with the Italians, whose peasant style of sanitation provided the fly with too frequent a paradise.'

Paying one's respect to the dead. Note the *Mückenschleier* (mosquito head net). As a captured German report grumbled: 'Plagues of flies and danger of infection are the inevitable results of any but most scrupulous cleanliness … The menace of flies cannot be exaggerated, as they convey the most serious diseases with which the armies in the field will have to contend.'

Emaciated yet cheerful *Afrikaner*. A combination of poor diet, poor sanitation and contaminated water left German troops extremely susceptible to jaundice and dysentery. As Rommel's adjutant noted on 24 May 1941: 'Scores of soldiers are sick. This number is increasing every day.' Another officer wrote, 'sometimes as many as sixty per cent of us suffer from dysentery-like diarrhoea at the same time. No one is spared. When you have it, you don't know whether you want to live or die.' Colonel Maximilian von Herff complained to Berlin: 'Gastric disorders – a kind of chill – are rife here. They occur about once a month and leave you very weak for a while. After three days of it recently I felt so bad that I fainted three times in one day…but I got over it without reporting sick. At any rate all of us Africa warriors, officers and men alike, will be glad to see the back of it. We say, Never again, Africa!' The vitamin-poor diet also lead to widespread inflammation of gum tissue and the loss of teeth. Between March and June 1941, Rommel lost 12,203 men. Of this number, 3,512 were casualties, the remainder reported as ill. In September 1941, 11,000 out of the 48,000 Germans in North Africa were reported as sick. The problem continued to escalate during 1942 with medical records listing 68,879 men reported as ill at some point in the year. Of this number, 28,488 were evacuated to Europe for treatment.

Goats were procured from Arabs and gazelle hunted for their meat. With fresh fruit and vegetables practically unknown in the desert, the main rations were sardines in oil, tinned sausages and tins of preserved meat. Embossed with the letters 'A.M.', short for *Administrazione Militaire*, German troops dubbed it *Alter Mann* (Old Man); the Italians derided it as *Asinus Mussolini* (Mussolini's Arse) or *Arabio Morte* (Dead Arab).

A proud huntsman stands over his desert prey. Rommel was also a keen hunter, wrote his aide-de-camp. Having shot a wild gazelle, Rommel 'flashed out a large hunting-knife and finished the job. He eviscerated the animal expertly, sawed off the horns, and had the carcass loaded.' The liver, Rommel noted in a letter to his wife, was delicious. From a different perspective, an increasingly intolerant Hans Joachim Schraepler wrote home that Rommel would only participate in hunting gazelle when a kill was a certainty, the barren loathsome desertscape 'without poetry'.

A spiralling desert whirlwind dwarfs a column of vehicles. Formed by hot air near the ground surface rising quickly through cooler, low-pressure air above it, the phenomenon can produce radio interference and strong electrical fields. 'Ask a member of the *Afrikakorps* after a few years what memories have remained most for him,' *Oberleutnant* Harald Kuhn questioned in his memoirs. 'Despite the happy tendency of people to quickly purge unpleasant things out of their memories, he would answer: sandstorms, torturous swarms of black flies and bleak monotony.' In place of propaganda photos depicting oases, palm groves, donkeys, camels, Arabs or images of Tripoli, Derna or Benghasi, the 'fighting sees none of that or only after months' should he visit a rear area. 'For him every day means a struggle against the adversity of this country and continuous demands anew a large measure of willpower.'

Chapter 4
Tropical Uniforms and Awards

Newly uniformed *Oberschütze* (Senior Rifleman) recruits wearing early pattern tunics with pleated pockets under scalloped flaps.

Newly kitted out for tropical service, this gloved recruit was photographed at a European barracks. A lieutenant in the 104 Panzer Grenadier Regiment detailed receiving his kit in July 1942: 'We drew our tropical clothing. I could hardly believe what wonderful things German soldiers got for war. I received as my most important bit of furniture a huge rubber sealed tropical chest. The contents were really precious – a tropical helmet, a tent, a mosquito net with carrying case, a face veil, a sleeping bag, a pair of desert boots, long trousers, short trousers, a pair of tropical shoes, breeches, coat, blouse, string vests, a body belt of lambs wool – here a little shake of the head – goggles and much, much more. Nobody thought about what would happen to these wonderful things in the future, to which was added a wonderful rucksack, blankets and the usual officers' accoutrements like binoculars, map case, pistol and pouch, etc. There are obviously no sharpshooters in Africa as we hadn't been given a steel helmet. Therefore, we thought that the red lined caps must be able to give us great protection.'

A final goodbye before the African adventure.

Waiting at a southern European airfield for passage to Libya.

The tropical uniform issued to the DAK was entirely different from those worn in Europe. Cut from watertight linen in a style reminiscent of the traditional uniforms worn by the former German colonial defence forces, it proved unsuitable both in style and material. The stiff material did not provide adequate protection against either heat or cold. The material absorbed moisture from the dew in the early mornings making the uniforms uncomfortable to wear. A wartime report by Major Ernst-Otto Ballerstedt complained that a 'light gabardine material would be most suitable.' He believed that the cut tunic was too much like a 'normal jacket' and that it 'should be more on the blouse pattern with the sleeves closed at the end by the wristbands. Trousers and shorts are too tight. The waistband should be wider and more elastic and provide more support for the internal organs.' British tropical uniforms made of pure wool, though dark in colour, were considered far more practical.

Portraits of newly arrived *Afrikaner*. Note the wearing of continental black leather *Marschstiefel* (jack boots) and leather belt, top left. Tunics issued to other ranks were identical to those worn by officers, the latter responsible for providing their identifying shoulder straps.

Toppe noted that the tropical Luftwaffe uniforms 'were good. Their colour, a yellowish-brown, was more appropriate than other German [army] uniforms, and they were made from a material that was of a lighter and better quality which was cut in a more appropriate style... Owing to the stiff material from which it was made, the German tropical shirts were inferior to the British ones.'

Useless in combat, *Tropenhelm* (tropical helmets) proved cumbersome and were quickly discarded by troops on the front line.

The Luftwaffe's version of the cloth-covered *Tropenhelm* was identical to the army one with the exception of the *Wappen* (shield) in the form of the flying eagle, *Hoheitsabzeichen*, on the left side.

In theory, wearing *kurze Hosen* (shorts) was forbidden during combat, since they left bare legs exposed to injury by thorns and stones. These superficial wounds led to bacterial skin infection characterised by hard, crusted sores over deep ulceration.

The iconic M1940 *Feldmütze mit Schirm* (tropical peaked cap) issued to the *Afrikakorps* was probably the most recognisable item of clothing in the desert. To emulate the appearance of the so-called '*alte Afrikaner*', new replacements arriving in 1942 would decolourise their caps using Losantin (a bleaching agent used to decontaminate skin burns arising from poisonous gas) tablets to resemble the sun-bleached desert veterans. Front line troops colloquially referred to the cap as an '*Afrikamütze*'.

Afrikakorps rank and file. Note the variation in head gear (including sand-painted helmets, officer's peaked cap and officer's version of the tropical M38 *Feldmütze*) and the death's head metal badges from the double-breasted black European Panzer jacket fastened on the lower lapel of the officer tunics.

A common myth amongst the Allied troops of the time was that the Germans had acclimatised their soldiers bound for Africa by marching them through giant hothouses designed to simulate desert conditions. In reality the first troops deployed received no specialised training apart from some basic educational lectures.

The double-breasted tropical greatcoat, cut from a dark brown woollen cloth in the same pattern as the continental version, was an essential clothing item in the desert. A number of senior German officers purchased leather greatcoats, detachable shoulder straps being the only insignia.

Motorcyclists received a tropical olive-coloured version of the double-breasted rubberised coat used in Europe. Note the divisional sign for the 21st Panzer Division on the BMW R 12 front mudguard beside the K-98 rifle.

On leave in Europe. The official service time in the desert for a German soldier was six months. Regular rotation, however, was not possible, resulting in many soldiers serving in the desert for twelve, even eighteen months. From the beginning Rommel was opposed to leave, believing that a rest home could instead be built along the coast for soldiers' wives to visit. But as his adjutant argued, 'recreation after a long deployment in another country is only possible at home. A holiday rest home would be nothing better than a brothel.' Within Germany, the tropical uniform was authorised for wear between 1 May and 30 September. Outside these dates, the regular field-grey continental was to be worn. A mix of uniform items, such as the wearing of black leather *Marschstiefel*, was prohibited.

Although Berlin sanctioned two percent of men on leave at any one time, Rommel protested that this figure was too high on account of the large number of men receiving medical treatment in Germany. With the total number of men absent from Africa capped at two percent, many of those troops in good health were denied leave.

Rommel arrived in Africa wearing the Pour le Mérite (Germany's highest First World War gallantry award) for his exploits against the Italians during the 1917 Battle of Caporetto. He was subsequently awarded the Knight's Cross with Oakleaves, for his actions commanding the 7th Panzer Division during the French Campaign, on 20 March 1941. He became a *Schwerterträger,* a recipient of the Knight's Cross with Oakleaves and Swords, on 20 January 1942, for actions in North Africa while commanding *Panzergruppe Afrika.* On 11 March 1943 he received the *Ritterkreuz des Eisernes Kreuzes mit Eichenlaub, Schwertern und Brillianten* (Knight's Cross of the Iron Cross with Oakleaves, Swords and Diamonds) for actions while commanding *Heersgruppe Afrika* in Libya and Tunisia.

Newly decorated with the Eisernes Kreuz 2. Klasse (Iron Cross 2nd Class).

Wearing the 'Afrikakorps' cuff title – an idea proposed by Rommel's adjutant Hans-Joachim Schraepler – was authorised on 18 July 1941 by *Generalfeldmarschall* Walther von Brauchitsch. A formation title rather than a campaign award, recipients needed two month's active service in Africa to be eligible. It was worn on the lower right sleeve, including continental tunics when home on leave. Schraepler proposed another award, a new medal between that would sit the Iron Cross First Class and the Knight's Cross. He also suggested a payment to soldiers enabling them to be able to later buy the decorations to which they were entitled.

Hitler authorised the introduction of the 'Afrika' cuff title on 21 January 1943. This campaign decoration replaced the original 'Afrikakorps' cuff title, which was to be removed. Army troops were eligible for the award based on three criteria: six months service in Africa; no time restriction was placed on individuals who had served in Africa and were decorated for bravery (such as the Iron Cross or German Cross in gold; individuals who had served longer than three months who were invalided back to Europe due to sickness were also eligible. All three requirements were waived if an individual was killed in action with the next of kin receiving the citation. A later Führer directive issued on 1 July 1943 reduced the period of active service to four months for service in the last months of the campaign in Tunisia. The award was worn on the lower left tunic sleeve.

This 'semi-official' Luftwaffe version of the 'Afrikakorps' cuff would be worn on leave during active service in North Africa and removed if transferred to another theatre. Provided the recipient was qualified, the individual would eventually receive the 'Afrika' Campaign Award cuff title. Note the German/Italian 'Afrika' Campaign ribbon on the tunic.

This Luftwaffe 'Afrika' cuff title was worn on the lower right cuff. It was awarded to Luftwaffe personnel serving in Africa from February 1942 to February 1943.

The Italian-German Campaign Medal in North Africa was introduced by the Italian Military specifically for German troops in early 1942. The medal featured the *Arco dei Felini*, flanked by the Italian fasces and German swastika, atop the Royal Knot of the House of Savoy, which was symbolic of brothers-in-arms. The reverse featured an armoured knight from each nation holding closed the jaws (the Suez Canal) of a crocodile (the British Empire). The wearing of all Italian awards was prohibited after 29 March 1944 following the collapse of Axis Italy. In the same way that the *Winterschlacht im Osten* 1941/42 (Eastern Front Medal) for troops serving in the Soviet Union was derided as the 'Order of the Frozen Flesh', so the Italian decoration was mocked as the 'Sardine Order', the 'Avanti Order' or the 'Sandstorm Order'.

Chapter 5
Zeltlager (Tent camp)

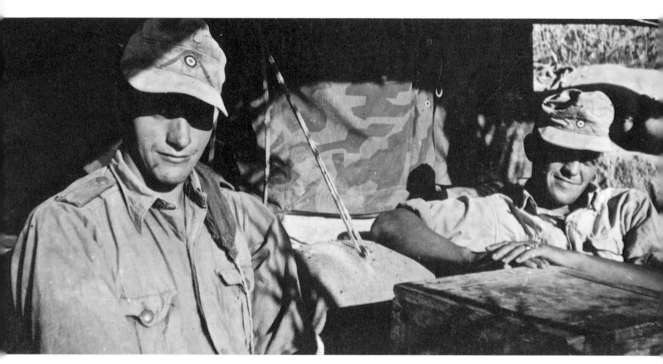

Describing life under canvas, the wartime photo book *Balkenkreuz über Wüstensand* recorded that tents are 'very practical and easily erected … one can imagine the beautiful wind blowing freshly through the tent. In reality the tents are only really useful in the daytime for hatching eggs!'

Schraepler detailed the discomfort of sleeping under canvas: '…there is a plethora of sand fleas, very small animals that you can feel when, full of blood and the size of peas, they abandon your body leaving fierce itching. The pioneers suffered most: the ones with bites swim in the sea, which is painful because of the strong salinity.'

At the beginning of the African campaign each soldier was issued with a one-man tent. Troops were later issued larger tents with awnings for additional protection from the sun.

Campsites were selected for their protection from aerial attack. Preference was given to depressions in the steep sides of the djebels, the banks of wadis and the dune areas, which offered the opportunity to dig in and camouflage vehicles and tents.

Wall tents for four men, with a double top awning, were used chiefly as shelter. They proved thoroughly useful and met all the requirements of desert warfare. There were also larger tents for ten or twelve men. However, these could be used for the most part only in rear areas, since it was practically impossible to camouflage them.

The coastal zone was often used as a bivouac area because it offered good opportunities for digging in tents and vehicles with usually good water-supply facilities. The only sections of the coast where there were no dunes were the cliff sections at Tobruk, Bardia and Sollum.

Every man was warned to be careful of scorpions, spiders and venomous snakes. Camping sites were to be carefully searched. 'The area is full of surprises', Schraepler declared; '… it is not infrequent to find these little things in your boots', another officer acknowledged.

Measures taken against temperature variations included warm clothing and bellybands worn after sunset. Each soldier was issued three blankets, one of which had to serve as a ground sheet for protection against night dew. Wounded men were given four blankets: two for covering and two for resting on.

Camel thorn bushes were used to break up the silhouette of a tent. 'The tropical heat and other inconveniences is making a lot of soldiers nervous,' Rommel's adjutant penned home. What each member of the Afrikakorps has to accept here in Africa is enormous.'

As well as newspapers from home, several front-line newspapers were produced including *Die Oasis* and *Die Karawane*. British war correspondent Alan Morehead noted: 'Where our men in the desert had not seen a newspaper for months, let alone any reading to divert and encourage their minds, the *Afrikakorps* were abundantly supplied. Every one of their camps I saw was strewn with recent magazines and pamphlets.'

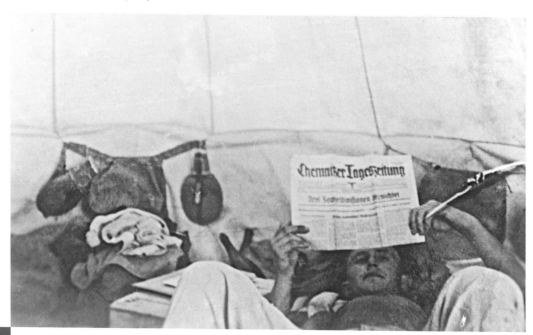

Washing and ironing were comparative luxuries, restricted mainly for those behind the front lines. In the absence of precious water, petrol was also used for washing. Troops in the line, according to a German doctor, would wash their clothes roughly twice in a two-month period. *Schwimmseife* (swim soap) in place of the regular army-issue soap was used to wash clothes in salty seawater.

A lull in the fighting, an opportunity to mend clothes.

Mail, according to Toppe, was 'Even more important than rations for the wellbeing of soldiers in the desert is the maintenance of regular communications with the zone of the interior. The word "mail" occupies a place of high priority in desert warfare. All officers and agencies must be concerned, therefore, with assuring a rapid distribution of mail to the front lines.' *Hauptmann* Wolfgang Evereth noted the efficiency of the *Feldpost* in a diary entry on 23 January 1942. After a day of fighting, '…a supply vehicle with the mail! A letter from my father dated 10 January already here. Juffa sent a postcard of snow-covered mountains. What a contrast!'

Balkenkreuz über Wüstensand enthused: '…because we are vain like all men and for some reason lay particular importance on being brown, we roll our socks down and run around whenever we can, at least half naked or even more so. So one can see us there, tanned and far from home.'

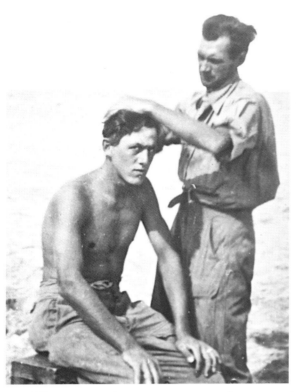

Alfresco grooming scenes, a source of amusement to some.

Water consumption in inland combat areas was generally limited, with washing an infrequent luxury.

Relaxing by the 'German swimming pool', as some members of the *Afrikakorps* dubbed the Mediterranean. Each soldier was issued with a pair of *Badehosen* (swimming trunks). Schmidt detailed, paradoxically, how men from the 15th Panzer Division, relieved from the stress of front-line service at Tobruk, suddenly became ill upon a period of rest beside the sea: 'The physical reaction among the men was immediate and patent. About seventy percent of the unit went down at once with diseases such as dysentery and jaundice. The fighting strength of the unit, which had always been above normal in the Tobruk line, was at once, reduced so gravely that companies were only of platoon effectiveness.'

'Our whole life and bustle are here quite simple and primitive, including meals,' Hans-Joachim Schraepler noted.

The to-and-fro movement of armies across the desert would have brought about economic devastation in a European state. Nomadic Bedouin, however, were barely affected and continued to graze their animals as they had done for centuries. Those near the busy coastal road watched the movement back and forth of various armies, holding up eggs for sale.

Fruit, whenever available, was a welcome addition to an inadequate diet fortified with vitamin pills.

A pet dog belonging to a *Kraftradfahrer*, pictured on his BMW R12. After the North African campaign, Field Marshal Bernard Montgomery named his pet spaniel after his vanquished opponent: 'Rommel'.

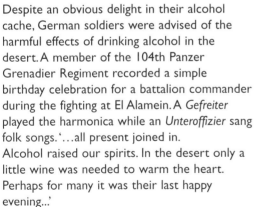

Despite an obvious delight in their alcohol cache, German soldiers were advised of the harmful effects of drinking alcohol in the desert. A member of the 104th Panzer Grenadier Regiment recorded a simple birthday celebration for a battalion commander during the fighting at El Alamein. A *Gefreiter* played the harmonica while an *Unteroffizier* sang folk songs. '…all present joined in. Alcohol raised our spirits. In the desert only a little wine was needed to warm the heart. Perhaps for many it was their last happy evening…'

Friedrich-Wilhelm von Mellenthin, an intelligence officer on Rommel's staff, wrote of the poor diet: 'for months we had no fresh vegetables and lived only on tinned stuff.' The *Feldkochbuch für warme Länder* (Field cook book for warm countries) was issued on 30 June 1942 based on experiences gained in the desert thus far. Unlike the double standard for Italian officers and ordinary troops, Rommel insisted that his officers share the same rations as their men.

Anhang 2 zur H. Dv. 1a
Seite 61, lfd. Nr. 14

Entwurf

Feldkochbuch
für
warme Länder

zum ständigen Gebrauch bei der Feldküche
zugleich zur Unterrichtung
der Kommandeure, Einheitsführer und Sanitätsoffiziere

vom 30. 6. 1942

A welcome addition to a monotonous diet – fresh mutton and pork. The eating of raw meat was prohibited and all slaughtered carcasses were supposed to be inspected by a medical officer.

'Our nourishment', recalled an officer in the 5th Panzer Regiment, 'was one of the saddest episodes of those months: bread, leathery meat in cans characterised by our soldiers as the "old man" – or canned sardines and dried vegetables; infrequently, a lemon for fresh vitamins. Day-by-day, week-by-week, month-by-month – always the same … in the supply depots in Bengazi and Tripoli there were better things on hand, donations from the homeland in the form of canned fruit, canned ham and other unknown pleasures – even, sparkling wine.'

The absence of trees and available firewood was a perennial problem in the desert. Wood was shipped to the treeless zone of battle from Italy.

A Henschel Type 33 truck pictured with a Hf. 14 *kleine Feldküche* (small field kitchen) converted for motorised towing.

A late model Hf. 14 *kleine Feldküche* fitted with the original storage compartment replaced with an additional roasting and stewing unit. Karl Rudolf Fissler invented the mobile field kitchen in 1892 to deliver hot meals to soldiers near the front.

With rations unaltered for African conditions, many Germans succumbed to sickness. According to war correspondent Hans von Esebeck, 'one of the reasons we had so much sickness, especially jaundice, was that our rations were too heavy for the desert … for the first four months we got no fresh vegetables at all. We lived all the time on Italian tinned meat.' Appropriated enemy stores, such as these cans of tinned fruit, were always welcomed.

28 April 1941. *Leutnant* Joachim Schorm jotted in his diary: 'We have now been away from Germany for two months and without butter, etc., into the bargain. Our principal food is bread, with something to spread on it. In this heat, every bite needs a sip of water or coffee to help it down. There is no fat.'

Toppe believed that 'soldiers should [ideally] observe a siesta,' whenever the situation permits. 'The daily routine in the desert did not substantially differ from that in other theatres of war. When not in combat, the troops were, as far as possible, given a lengthy rest period during the great heat around noon. The maintenance troops (workshop companies) were also given a noon rest period. Supply traffic could not afford to take these rests.'

Afrikaner gather around a Blaupunkt-designed WR1 *Wehrmacht-Rundfunkempfänger.* Shortwave services broadcast by the *Reichs-Rundfunk-Gesellschaft* were best received in the mid-afternoon to early evening. Norbert Schultze's *Lied eines Jungen Wachtposten,* otherwise known as Lili Marlene, was an immensely popular song on both sides. Hans-Joachim Schraepler penned that he 'did not realise how it might be a kind of meeting point for the thoughts and feelings we have for those who are dear to us in Germany.' Even Hitler was an admirer, declaring 'not only will this song delight the German soldier, it will certainly outlive us all.'

Tanned troops relax to the music of a regimental band. Music was an important facet of German national identity, recognised as the 'most German art'.

Troops making their own entertainment. The Allies later instituted strict and repressive 'Music Control' on Germany following the fall of the Third Reich in May 1945. Only music 'incidental to services of a religious character' was initially allowed, with public performances of songs and military marches associated with the Army or Nazis forbidden.

Music and horseplay offered an escape from the privations of soldiering.

Chapter 6
1941

Rommel arrived in Tripoli on 12 February 1941 with orders to act as a *Sperrverband* to bolster the Italians after their recent rout by the British. He was uncertain whether his tanks could actually manoeuvre across the sandy terrain, as Italian sources had indicated, or even if his ordinary wheeled vehicles could successfully operate in such an unfamiliar environment.

In conference with Generals Ludwig Crüwell and Alfred Gause. On meeting Rommel for the first time, his aide-de-camp, Heinz Werner Schmidt, recalled: 'His figure is compact and short. I gain a measure of confidence as I note that, although I am only of middle height, the General is shorter. He gives me a brief, powerful shake of the hand. Blue-grey eyes look steadily into mine … His mouth and chin are well formed and strong, and reinforce my first impression of an energetic, vital personality.'

The first German units to arrive in Africa in February 1941 received no information about the nature of the desert. Minimal intelligence data furnished by the Italians was compounded by inaccurate maps. Captured British maps, accordingly, were especially prized. 'Cooperation with our Italian allies is too difficult,' Rommel's adjutant penned. 'Everything has to be considered down to the smallest detail and to be harmonised.'

The German 8.8cm *Flugzeugabwehrkanone* (or Flak) 18/36/37 gun was probably the most well-known artillery piece of the war. Disadvantaged by its high silhouette, the weapon, nevertheless, could be brought quickly into action and was fearsome in the hands of an experienced crew against Allied tanks over long distances.

Panzerkampfwagen, Panzer for short and abbreviated as Pz.Kpfw., literally means 'armoured fighting vehicle'. The crew of this Pz.Kpfw. III *Ausführung*, or Ausf. H clean grit and powder residue from the barrel of the 5.0cm main gun. Frequent maintenance was needed to protect the vehicle from the effects of sand and dust with engine life considerably shortened despite the addition of large air filters.

The Germans were quick to censure their Italian allies after their abortive campaign against Egypt. According to Siegfried Westphal: 'It would be superficial to simply dismiss the Italian soldier as a failure … the real causes lay much deeper, and some of them should be brought to light. Neither the armed forces nor the people had any inspiring war aim before their eyes. At home the soldier found no moral support. Nor was he equipped or prepared for war with a European opponent armed with all the weapons that modern technique could supply. This was why his achievements, taken as a whole, were less than those in the First World War.'

The penetrating power of Italian anti-tank weapons, and the 'range, calibre and sighting of its artillery, including anti-aircraft guns, were all inferior,' noted Westphal. 'A considerable proportion of the guns had been part of the booty captured at the time of the collapse of Austria-Hungary in the autumn of 1918 …' A half-truth, many guns in service were also pre-1914 Italian pieces such as this cannone da 75/27 mod. 1911, a French field gun manufactured by Déport.

'The Italian Army's tank forces were particularly lacking in armour, fire-power and ability to traverse rough country,' Westphal continued. The vehicle on the left is an Italian L3/35 tankette, armed with twin 8mm machine guns.

The 13.5-ton Italian M13/40 medium tank was armed with a 47mm main gun and protected by 25 to 42mm of bolted armour plate. Powered by Fiat SPA V-8 diesel engine, it carried a crew of four. Note the missing return roller.

Comrades in arms. Camouflaged Italian field gun and crew in a photo likely taken by Rommel. Rainer Kriebel, DAK staff officer, recorded that the Italians 'felt very bitter about their very inferior equipment and armament'.

Fiat 1100L 'Camioncino', produced from 1938 to 1941 in the foreground. The vehicle behind is most likely a Fiat 626. Both images on this page were likely taken by Rommel, a keen photographer.

After flying over the desert, a Luftwaffe general wrote in April 1941 that: 'Mobility is restricted almost entirely to the desert road…the further east you go along the desert road, the more inhospitable the landscape becomes: while for about thirty miles east of Benghazi the colonising work of the Italians is evident, around Derna and Tobruk there are no signs of human habitation. Even the pitiful stunted pines fall off. The thorny shrubs struggle up to knee height.' More ominously, Hans-Joachim Schraepler confided in a letter home the same month that the 'supply of our troops is not in step with our advance.'

1932 Lancia Astura, one of many civilian cars brought across from Europe.

Command vehicles: a pair of Opel Admiral four-door cabriolets operating in an environment never intended.

One of several Sd.Kfz. 250/3 *leichter Funkpanzerwagen* used by Rommel, this one named after the mythical *Greif* ('Griffin'). 'The general', one of Rommel's staff officers noted, 'feels the urge to meet the men who are face to face with the enemy. He has to speak with them, crawl forward to them in their foxholes, and have a chat with them.' He knew, von Mellenthin observed, 'how to make them feel somehow immortal'.

A *Leichter Panzerspähwagen* Sd.Kfz. 221 photographed at Mersa al Brega on 31 March 1941. A total of 339 of these armoured cars were built from 1935 to 1940.

Rommel was 'boiling with impatience' upon arriving in Africa, Westphal recalled. The future 'Desert Fox' 'radiated energy'. 'I have never met anyone until now as agile in thinking and acting as him,' his adjutant, Hans-Joachim Schraepler, wrote on 9 March. 'He is fully engaged by the fulfilment of his mandate, he sets an example rarely encountered.'

Rommel found that the Italians in Tripoli were dubious about his mission to defend Tripolitania. A reconnaissance flight over the unknown country helped him to formulate plans for what became an offensive to reach the Nile Delta.

Fixed defences under construction. Frequently airborne in his Fieseler Fi 156 *Storch*, Rommel landed amongst a missing armoured column on 7 April to reprove their progress and detour around a large body of water – an oasis. *Oberleutnant* Harald Kuhn wrote of Rommel touring the 'battlefield as cool as a cucumber…even though the airspace was swarming with English fighters.'

Westphal: 'In twelve days he [Rommel] had won back everything that General Wavell had taken fifty days to capture – with one exception. The German divisions were too weak, even with the help of Italian reinforcements, to take Tobruk, which the British still occupied. Numerous attempts to overrun the fortress were defeated by the determined resistance of the defenders, as well as by the exhaustion and weakness of the attackers ... There were now two fronts: one to the east along the Sollum-Bardia line, the other a strength-sapping siege around Tobruk. There could be no question but that this fortress should be the immediate object of the operations of both opponents.'

Originally a civilian design, the BMW R 12 was one of the most widely used German motorcycles in the Wehrmacht.

Enemy booty. This British AEC Armoured Command Vehicle carrying a *Balkenkreuz* was one of three British AEC 'Dorchester' armoured command vehicles captured near Mechili on 7-8 April 1941. Rommel and his staff subsequently used two of these spacious vehicles, nicknamed 'Moritz' and 'Max'.

The tell-tale sign of mechanised movement in the desert. Rommel used dust clouds for camouflage and deception up until the summer of 1942, though he too fell victim to equivalent enemy deception measures. Schraepler noted the difficulty of operating in the desert. 'In France, for example, we could always find food or petrol, even vehicles, which could be used instead of our own vehicles which had broken down.'

Schmidt recorded the approach to battle: 'we headed straight for the enemy tanks. I glanced back. Behind me was a fan of vehicles – a curious assortment of all types – spread out as far as the eye could see. There were amoured troop carriers, cars of various kinds, caterpillars hauling mobile guns, heavy trucks with infantry, motorised anti-aircraft guns …' The eight-wheeled armoured car in the centre is a Sd.Kfz. 231 (8-rad) *Schwerer Panzerspähwagen* (heavy reconnaissance armored car).

A miscellany of wheeled and tracked vehicles. On the far right is an Austrian Saurer RR-7/2, known in the Wehrmacht as the *mittlerer gepanzerter Beobachtungskraftwagen* Sd.Kfz. 254. A total of 128 of these armoured observation vehicles were manufactured. If required, the wheels were retracted for tracked cross-country movement.

All eyes on the horizon. To the left of the Sd.Kfz. 250/3 half-track is a Sd.Kfz. 10 1-ton halftrack, designed to tow a light artillery piece or a trailer. Six manufacturers produced some 25,000 Sd.Kfz. 10 vehicles during the course the war.

'Sandstorms', wrote one British correspondent, 'blew indifferently upon Germans and British'. They could, however, prove advantageous. During the German attack on Tobruk on 12 April, the weather obscured all movement outside the perimeter so, Rommel noted, 'there was no need to concern ourselves about aimed British artillery fire.'

Tank combat often proved difficult in the mid-afternoon, the hottest time, because of the effect of desert heat haze on weapon optics. A different problem arose hours later when the setting sun silhouetted vehicles against the sky.

Derna was captured on 8 April 1941. Rommel harried his men to continue onward to Tobruk. The sign on the old Turkish wall declares: *Selbständiges Quartiermachen verboten! Quartierzuweisung beim Standortkommandanten* (It is forbidden to arrange quarters by yourself! Allocation of quarters by the garrison commander). The panels below the Derna sign read: *Sanitätspark* (Heer) = ambulance (army); *Heereslazarett* I = Army hospital; *Feldlabor* (Heer) = field laboratory (army).

Battle-scarred Fort Capuzzo. Situated near the Libyan-Egyptian frontier, the former Italian fort changed hands numerous times during the Desert War. Reflecting on the fall of the fort on 16 May 1941, Rommel's adjutant penned that the 'fighting in the desert is really particularly bitter. We don't think anybody at home can imagine it...'

Fort Acroma, 30 kilometres west of Tobruk, under new ownership. The Battalion History of *Panzer-Aufklärungs-Abteilung* 33 provides a telling insight into the difficulties encountered: 'At 0700 hours on 7 May, the battalion moved out from its rest area in the vicinity of the fork in the Tobruk-Acroma road and headed south. We reached the desert fort of Acroma moving along a trail that was completely filled with numerous potholes. Following that, we continued south-southeast. Keeping a distance of 10 kilometres [6 miles] from the outer defensive belt around Tobruk, we moved in the direction of the crossroads of trails at El Adem. There, we turned to the east, with a march objective of the airfield at Gambut. After passing the reference point of Sidi Rezegh, the battalion ran into difficulties. We got lost in the trackless and – at least to us – completely foreign desert landscape. We were forced to halt again and again. The *ghibli* from the previous day had completely covered up the tracks from vehicles. There were no trees or vegetation, let alone any directional signs of even the most primitive type. There was only sand, rock and the occasional hardwood dried-out camel thorn bush. The heat juggled objects and sections of terrain through a *fata morgana* [mirage], which made it even more difficult for us – inexperienced in desert warfare – to get oriented…'

German columns reached Bardia, just visible in the distance, on 9 April before crossing the Egyptian frontier. Pictured beside the Via Balbia is a 1936 Ford with civilian number plates.

'Bardia', wrote Heinz Schmidt, 'is perched on the edge of a precipitous cliff overlooking the Mediterranean, with an almost land-locked bay – the resort of ancient pirates a thousand years ago – far below on its eastern hand … Rommel found it a good Advance HQ, for it provided comfort for strenuous work and was convenient for a commander who believed in close contact with his troops.'

Battle was depicted in many soldiers' photo albums as distant explosions against the horizon in a largely mobile contest. The positional warfare fought during the 1941 siege of Tobruk, however, was a form of combat for which German troops were neither prepared nor familiar with from their earlier campaigns in Europe. Indeed, Rommel attributed the more than 1,200 casualties suffered during the May 1941 attack on Tobruk to the passage from open to static warfare.

The detritus of war. An early version of the *mittlerer geländegängiger Personenkraftwagen* (Kfz.12) or *m. gl. Einheits-Pkw* (medium cross-country passenger car). The vehicle was manufactured by Horch, Wanderer and Opel from 1937 to 1943.

A badly shredded British Guy Quad Ant field artillery tractor (FAT). Approximately 4,000 of these British vehicles were produced from 1938 to 1944.

'From a purely technical point of view', Toppe explained, 'it is extremely difficult to prepare field fortifications in the North African steppes and desert. Wherever the ground in the steppes is stony, it is very hard, because there is a layer of so-called surface chalk on the surface. This layer is formed when the rainwater absorbed during the winter rises to the surface again during the summer and evaporates. During this process, the dissolved matter, such as chalk, silicic acid, etc., is separated again and cements the top layers into a firm crust, having a thickness of from fifty centimetres to two meters. Under this surface chalk layer, there is a so-called lixiviation stratum that is especially soft and therefore easier to work.'

'Our boys are tired,' Rommel confided to Schraepler on 4 May. Writing home the next day, the latter complained of the 'permanent shelling' by the British artillery, confiding that 'none of our fronts demand so much of our soldiers … here there is a shortage of everything. Even the way of fighting is different. We have had more losses … an indication of the seriousness of the fighting.'

The *Schwerer Panzerspähwagen* Sd.Kfz. 232 'Fu' (*Funkapparat*, or radio apparatus) 8-rad was the command-radio variant of the Sd.Kfz. 231 heavy armoured car. Note the large frame aerial above turret, housing a 2.0cm cannon and MG 34 machine gun.

The Germans first encountered the heavily armoured, slow moving British Infantry Tank Mark II, known as the 'Matilda', during in the Battle of Arras in France on 21 May 1940. Rommel, then commander of the 7th Panzer Division, recalled that he halted the enemy advance by personally directing the fire of every available anti-tank and 8.8cm Flak gun against the oncoming British tanks.

Like the Matilda, this knocked out British Cruiser Mark IV (A13 Mk II) was also armed with the 2-pounder gun. Lighter and faster than the infantry tanks, which were intended to support advancing infantry, the British Cruiser class of tanks were designed for mobile warfare. Unlike German and Italian doctrine that instructed crews to fire when stationary, even in the open desert, it was standard practice for British tankers to fire on the move except when firing in hull-down firing positions.

Captured British Universal Carriers saw service in the *Afrikakorps* as the Bren 731(e). This scrutinised example is armed with both a Bren gun and a Boys anti-tank rifle.

'Because of the danger of flooding, most of the highway [the Via Balbia] runs along a causeway,' Max Reisch recalled. 'Alas, many a valuable vehicle went tumbling over because they went too near the verges when overtaking or giving way. The edge of the road looked safe and firm enough but it was as treacherous as the desert itself.'

Vormarsch! The upturned walking stick symbol with a small 7 identifies the car from the Luftwaffe *Kreigsberichter Kompanie* (mot.) 7.

Australian troops – part of the besieged garrison Germany's Lord Haw Haw derided as the 'rats' of Tobruk – of the 2/48th Battalion transport section inside the fortress pose before a captured Fiat 626 NLM (Nafta Lungo Militare) medium truck.

Tobruk

By mid-April Rommel had recovered all territory lost in Operation Compass and pushed British forces back 500 miles (800km) to the Egyptian frontier with one exception: the coastal port Tobruk, which the Italians had strongly fortified. Rommel was unsuccessful in overcoming the spirited defence during a series of clashes in mid-April 1941 known as the 'Easter Battles'. A subsequent attack on 30 April-1 May also failed, thwarting his plan to reach the Suez Canal. In some of the most intense fighting of the campaign, German forces managed only to occupy a portion of the western perimeter, known as 'The Salient'. Siege warfare was particularly depressing for those troops who had fought in the swiftly moving Battle of France in 1940. It was believed that morale inside Tobruk was poor and that the fortress would easily succumb once the perimeter was pierced. In mid-April, one German solider noted: 'They already have a lot of dead and wounded in the 3rd Company. It is very distressing. In their camp faces are very pale and all eyes … downcast. Their nerves are taunt to breaking point.' After visiting the front lines in May 1941, General Friedrich Paulus (later to surrender the German Sixth Army at Stalingrad) complained that the 'troops around Tobruk are fighting in conditions that are inhuman and intolerable. I am going to recommend to Berlin that we withdraw to a strong position at Gazala, where our supply lines will be shorter. The troops will live under better conditions, and we should be ensured greater reserves … As I see it, every man here is on duty without a break.'

Other elderly vehicles abandoned by retreating Italian forces at Tobruk included this Pavesi Model P4-100 Artillery Tractor (above) and a late model SPA 25C *Autoambulanza* (below).

Captured Italian coastal artillery. This *cannone da* 149/47 Skoda was photographed at Tobruk.

An Australian infantryman poses next to a captured *cannone da* 120 / 45. The original caption places the gun at Halfaya Pass near the Egyptian frontier.

Numerous captured Italian artillery pieces, such as this Italian *cannone da* 47/32 with improvised shield, were pressed into service by Australian infantry – the so-called 'Bush Artillery'. One of the first kills by the amateur gunners, in concert with British 25-pounder guns, was *Generalmajor* Heinrich von Prittwitz und Gaffron, recently arrived at the front on 10 April ahead of the 15th Panzer Division.

Moving into battle. It was a depressing experience for the new troops of the 15th Panzer Division, who were flown directly into Derna and thrust into the front line. Rather than a romantic image of desert palms, reality was an arid, stony battlefield more closely resembling the trench systems of the First World War. These men, Schmidt noted, 'hated the Africa they saw.' Fighting in the desert, Schraepler observed, imposed 'hardships, which one cannot imagine in Germany …'

A disassembled German *SchrappnellMinen*-35 ('S'-mine). Upon triggering the three-pronged pressure fuse, a cylinder was propelled approximately a metre into the air before a high explosive charge dispersed some 360 steel balls with deadly effect.

A German NCO recalled how 'sometimes it was a gentlemanly war; when we besieged Tobruk we were laying mines outside Tobruk, and in the darkness a voice said, "what are you doing here?" To our surprise one of our soldiers answered, "We are laying mines." The British answered calmly, "That's exactly what we are doing." Both sides went on laying mines, not shooting at each other; and left in the end.'

The German Teller 35 mine (T.Mi.35) was a metal-cased anti-tank mine. Instructions called for the mines to be laid from 80 to 100mm (3 to 4 inches) below the surface to prevent sympathetic detonation. Likewise, the mines might not function if they were lower than 100mm (4 inches) below the surface.

Junkers Ju 87 B-2 or *Stuka* (from *Sturzkampfflugzeug*, meaning 'dive bomber') aircraft were also flown by Italian pilots in North Africa where they were known as the *Picchiatello* (or Crazy Diver).

Tobruk's harbour was heavily targeted, with 787 air raids recorded in the first three months of the siege alone. The dogged defence of Tobruk, 100 miles (160km) behind the front, denied Rommel from using the harbour as a forward port for his supplies. British offensives to relieve the fortress (Operations Brevity and Battleaxe, May and June 1941) both failed.

Supply quickly became a chronic problem for the *Afrikakorps*, one that only intensified the further from Tripoli Rommel's columns advanced. Schraepler wrote of the myriad of problems in a letter home on 8 May 1941: 'There are enormous difficulties with supplies. Sometimes this is missing, sometimes that. We always lack loading capacity. A large load of supplies has arrived in Tripoli, but we could not transport it. Lately the Arabs have refused to unload ships, because some time ago, planes bombed and killed some of their compatriots … several units have arrived without vehicles but cannot be transported to the front. This explains why we have a lot of problems in the field.' A letter written the following day expounded how 'transporting is time consuming and costs material. In addition, there are losses of ships while crossing between Italy and Tripoli, and into the port of Tripoli. The Italians don't do anything. They have no planes and no fleet to fight in the Mediterranean. It is depressing … The Englishman is a cool calculator. He knows that he can leave us in peace at the front, when cutting supplies behind. Berlin has no idea of these problems.'

Armour lost in the 'Easter Battles' at Tobruk, a Pz.Kpfw I Ausf. B (above) and Pz.Kpfw. III Ausf. J (below). A contemporary German report on the Pz.Kpfw I, which initially made up a quarter of Rommel's armoured strength, dismissed it as too weak, too slow and totally unsuitable for the Western Desert.

The grim reality of war. Dead gunners beside their 5.0cm *Panzerabwehrkanone* (Pak) 38 (L/60).

A knocked-out 8.8cm Flak 36 and Sd.Kfz 7 half-track. Fearsome in the hands of an experienced crew, the '88' could knock out the formidably armoured British Matilda at ranges up to 2,000 yards with a practiced crew firing up to twenty rounds a minute. Note the lowered outriggers. The *Sonderhanger* 201 (special suspension 201) limber enabled the gun to be fired while still on its wheels. Used in a field role at Tobruk firing time-fused HE air-burst, as one Australian infantryman complained, the gun was 'anti-everything'.

Heavy artillery. The 15cm *schwere Feldhaubitze* model 18, or sFH 18, was the standard German Army howitzer with service long after the Second World War in a number of countries, including Czechoslovakia, Finland and parts of Central and South America.

Development of the Italian *cannone da 149-35* began in 1896. Lacking a recoil system, wooden ramps and wheel belts were used instead to absorb the recoil energy. The fixed carriage mounting also deprived the gun from the ability to traverse. Despite its age, in the absence of more modern large calibre pieces, 923 were still in service in June 1940.

This Ju 87, forced down inside Tobruk, quickly became a target for souvenir hunters, as was the Fiat CR.42 Falco (falcon) pictured below. Note the missing fuselage and tail insignia. The CR.42, which first flew in 1938, stemmed from Italian interest in the achievements of biplanes in the Spanish Civil War.

Former Austro-Hungarian 8cm *Feldkanone* M 05 field guns, either captured or obtained through war reparations, became the Italian *cannone da* 77/28 mod. 5. The German designation for the gun was 7.65cm FK 5/8(ö) or (i). These veteran pieces were pressed into service as makeshift anti-tank guns.

Rommel monitors German gunners on a Ceirano 50CMA truck mounting a 75/27 CK (*Commissione Krupp*), *autocannone da* 75/27 C.K. anti-aircraft gun at a flat trajectory coastal shoot. A number of these vehicles were employed by the Germans in both anti-aircraft and anti-tank roles.

The 5.0cm Pak 38 replaced the 3.7cm Pak 36 during the summer of 1941. It was the fundamental responsibility of German anti-tank guns to engage British tanks, not panzers. All German armour-piercing ammunition above 3.7cm in calibre was available with both high-explosive and delay-fuse options. Upon striking a British tank, these projectiles were frequently associated with irreparable mechanical damage and horrendous injuries to the crew, unlike solid-shot, which often wounded the occupants but rarely destroyed the tank through fire or severe damage.

German 3.7cm Pak 36 anti-tank guns were widely exported before the outbreak of war. In Italian service they were known as the *Cannone contracarro da 37/45*. The gun was copied by the Japanese as the Type 97 and also influenced the design of the US Army's M3 anti-tank Gun.

In a ceremony held on 11 May 1941, flanked by German and Italian armour, Italo Gariboldi decorated Rommel with Italy's highest Gallantry award: the Military Order of Savoy, Grand Officer. On his chest Rommel wears the Italian Silver Bravery Medal, awarded earlier to him on 22 April 1941.

Helping to stage the event, Rommel's adjutant wrote: 'I positioned two tanks on either side of the two men [Rommel and Gariboldi]. On the left the Italians, the Germans on the right; it offered a good view of the ceremony to the cameramen and photographers.'

September 1941, Rommel and a cadre of Axis officers inspect a battery of German 10.5cm *Schwere Kanone* 18 (10.5cm K 18) guns targeting Tobruk. The gun was a composite design using a two-wheeled carriage designed by Krupp (the same as the 15cm sFH 18) with a barrel and breach designed by Rheinmetall.

An early version of the US manufactured Curtis P40, known as the Tomahawk II, of the British Desert Air Force (DAF).

The Hawker Hurricane was the DAF's other primary fighter aircraft during 1941. A hero of the Battle of Britain, later models gained a new lease of life in the Western Desert as a ground attack aircraft.

Messerschmitt Bf 109 'Yellow 4' of *Jagdgeschwader* 27, shot down near Tobruk. Aerial combat over North Africa produced some of Germany's leading 'Western Front' aces, such as Hauptman Hans-Joachim Marseille (151 kills over the desert) and *Oberleutnant* Hans-Arnold Stahlschmidt (59 desert kills) and *Leutnant* Gunther Steinhausen (40 desert kills).

Two captured Morris Commercial trucks. British experience in modern desert warfare began during the First World War and continued through the 1920s and 1930s. In 1937 Colonel Baron Geyr von Schweppenburg, the German military attaché in London, inspected the British garrison in Egypt. Praising the garrison's training, his insightful report declared that the natural obstacles of the Western Desert aided the defence of Egypt and that motorised troops were essential for offensive operations. He also believed that the British would be fully capable of supplying themselves via the Cape. His prophetic report concluded that 'any [Axis] offensive from the West must come to a halt on the Nile if not before.'

A captured Daimler Scout Car. This rugged and fast four-wheel drive reconnaissance vehicle was known as a 'Dingo'.

The Junkers Ju 52 performed an invaluable service, ferrying troops and supplies across the Mediterranean and bringing the sick and wounded back to Europe for medical care. A soldier of the 5th Panzer Regiment, 21st Panzer Division, recalled his journey to Africa: 'We (crew and tanks) were sent to Naples. Our tanks were to be shipped to Africa … We were to fly over in a flight of Ju 52s … The pilots were very nervous, they did not like the run. They basically threw us in the planes and took off. We flew only about 200 feet above the water.'

Despite local successes, supply shortages after weeks of fighting during Operation Crusader forced Rommel to fall back to El Agheila. Once again, British forces were unable to press onward to Tripoli, this time by Japan's entry into the war and the need to transfer men and equipment to the Far East. Meanwhile, two Axis convoys slipped safely across the Mediterranean without incident on 18 December 1941 and 5 January 1942. Replenished and reinforced, while Auchinleck was busy rebuilding his Middle East command, Rommel once again set his sights on a new 1942 offensive.

Chapter 7
Gefallene Kameraden
(Fallen Comrades)

The transport of the wounded was often carried out over great distances. Fieseler Fi 156 *Storch* (Stork) aircraft were available to carry head and stomach casualties from the advanced air stations to the medical installations in the rear. This was an ideal method of transportation because of its speed and the protection given to the wounded. Ju 52 medical aircraft (pictured) were also available for transport of the sick and wounded. Medical officers in combat units had an ambulance and a medical equipment truck.

Italian-supplied field hospital tents. The authorised strength of medical personnel and vehicles in Africa was twice that allowed for Europe. (The field kitchen in the foreground is a Hf. 13.)

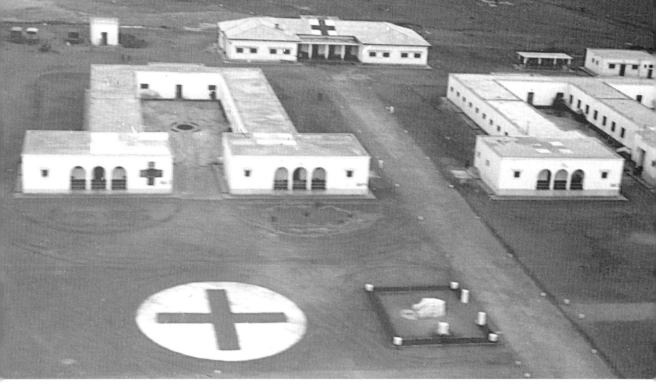

Clearly marked Axis hospital. Hans-Joachim Schraepler complained in a letter home (2 October 1941) of the RAF having 'systematically bombed military hospitals', including the one at Bardia and two more situated beside the Via Balbia.

Bengasi: signs to the *Kfz Sammelstelle* (motor vehicle assembly point) and *Heereslazarett II* = Army hospital.

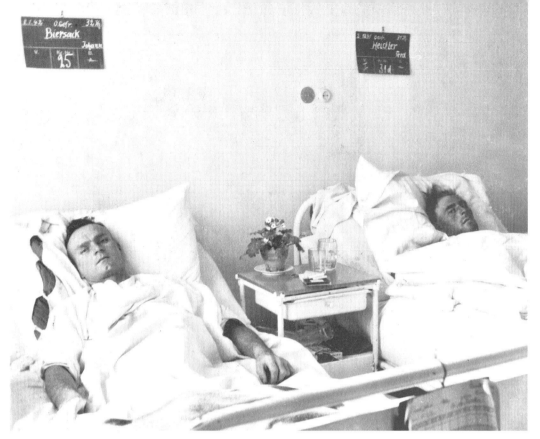

Stern-faced *Obergefreite* bed-ridden in a hospital ward, early 1942. Rommel's adjutant recalled a visit to a hospital in June 1941, '… causing a lot of joy to the soldiers with serious injuries and to the amputees. We had seen some shocking cases' as well as a large number of soldiers stricken with dysentery.

Convalescing *Afrikaner*. The Red Cross nurse in the centre wears the continental uniform in place of the tropical tan-coloured uniform.

The funeral service and burial of an unknown *Afrikaner*. A Catholic chaplain would typically wear a vestment over his tunic.

Zur Erinnerung im Gebete

an den Gefreiten

Georg Ganzerer

in einer Flak-Abteilung

welcher bei den schweren Kämpfen in Afrika am 15. Juli 1942 im Alter von 22 Jahren für sein Vaterland den Heldentod gestorben ist.

Meine Lieben, euch mußte ich verlassen
Um zu ziehen in's Feindesland
Ich mußte mein junges Leben lassen
Für Gott, Führer u. das liebe Vaterland

Ach, wir mußten Abschied nehmen
Und reichten uns zum letztenmal die Hand
Hier sehen wir uns niemals wieder
Doch hoffen wir's in einem schöneren Land

Buchdruckerei Gg. Hochhuber in Viechtach.

Sterbebild (Death Card) for 22-year-old *Grefreiten* Georg Ganzerer, a member of a Flak battalion killed in 'heavy fighting in Africa on 15 July 1942'. The custom of distributing *Sterbebild* most likely originated in Holland in the beginning of the eighteenth century to honour soldiers killed in battle. The cards would be given out to the visitors to a funeral and to relatives of the deceased. The poem on this card reads:

My dears, I had to leave you
to march into enemy's country.
I had to give my young life
for god, Führer and fatherland.

Oh, we had to say farewell
and shaked hands the last time
here we will see us never again
but, so we hope, in a better land.

Gefallene Kameraden. Memorial to the fallen of the 5th Light Division.

Gefreiter Werner Mork recounted his first experience of death following a British air attack: 'The old hands collected the dead as they wanted to them to Matruh, rather than bury them on the side of the road. Unfortunately, however, there was not enough room for all the bodies – it was far more important to transport the living instead of a pile of corpses. The dead no longer counted … It was an appalling experience, my first of this sort, and it revealed the war in its full ferocity and horror.'

German casualties in the North African theatre totalled 18,594 killed and 3,400 missing.

Rommel pictured at the cemetery outside Tobruk, September 1941. A war correspondent, possibly present on this occasion, wrote: 'That long summer of 1941 the war cemetery here swelled to quite a size and in the eerie twilight of a sandstorm it seemed to us, in all its cruel loneliness, something of a man's transience. We were looking at the grave of an officer. For a while he [Rommel] stood there, absolutely motionless. Then he turned away without a word and left … It was the sorrow of a man saying farewell to an old friend and comrade.'

Chapter 8
1942

Pz.Kpfw. IV Ausf. F2 (Sd.Kfz. 161), 8th Panzer Regiment. Armed with a long barrel 7.5cm KwK 40 L/43 gun, the tank was popularly known to the British as the 'Mark IV Special'.

An abandoned Maybach HL 120 TRM V-12 engine from either a Pz.Kpfw. III or IV. Operating without appropriate air filters halved the average life of a tank engine – a problem compounded by the need to operate in low gear for extended periods. Without special lubricants, Rommel's panzers needed an overhaul after 600 to 900 miles – the distance from Tripoli to Tobruk – and an engine replacement after only 2,100 miles (3,380 km), compared to 5,000 miles (8,500 km) under European conditions.

Geländemarsch (Cross-country march). Vehicles of the 21st Panzer Division's Reconnaissance Battalion push into Egypt in June 1942.

The Italian *Semovente da* 75/18 self-propelled gun incorporated the *Obice da* 75/18 *modello* 34 mountain gun on the chassis of a M13/40 or M14/41 tank. Despite its cramped interior, the vehicle performed well and production continued under German supervision after the Italian armistice. A total of 262 were built.

The US manufactured M3 Grant tank came as a shock to the Germans. Armed with a hull-mounted 75mm gun and a turret-mounted 37mm gun, it first saw combat in the desert at the Battle of Gazala in May 1942. Although hampered by the limited traverse of the main gun and the inability to fire from a hull down position, the 75mm gun fired both armour piercing and high explosive ammunition.

The 242 Grant tanks received by the 8th Army were evenly distributed among armoured regiments rather than concentrating them as a single offensive force. As a consequence some regiments had barely acquired their new tanks when Rommel launched his latest offensive. Note the symbol on the front mudguard: a red jerboa on a white background within a red square – the symbol of the British 7th Armoured Division.

An Italian Fiat 626 NLM medium truck approaches a knocked out Grant apparently abandoned on a rail crossing at Matruh.

Shot-up Marmon-Herrington, MK III Armoured Car from the 4th South African Armoured Car Regiment.

Another British victim, this time a burnt out Daimler Mk I armoured car.

Deception in the desert. German troops examine a dummy rail line and gun position, most likely constructed by the South African 85th Camouflage Company, South African Engineering Corps.

A knocked-out British Valentine Mk III. Classed as an 'Infantry Tank', the reliable Valentine was less heavily armoured than the Matilda and armed with the same 2-pounder gun. Remarkably, some vehicles of the 23rd Armoured Brigade were driven 3,000 miles (4,830km) on their on own tracks in the westward pursuit of the *Afrikakorps* after El Alamein without breaking down.

Crushing rock for a road surface under the harsh desert sun. The grill-less lorry is likely a German Model 1939 3-ton Ford.

Pz.Kpfw. III Ausf. L. The British practice of withdrawing into a leaguer stood in contrast to the German doctrine of recovery crews remaining on the battlefield. Immobilised vehicles from both sides could be either recovered and repaired, or destroyed.

Vehicle workshop. Wolfgang Everth (5th Light Division) wrote of the chronic vehicle shortage in Africa in January 1942: 'Parties sent out to salvage captured trucks, guns and ammunition – things we urgently needed … Fourteen of my vehicles are back in workshops and can't be repaired because of the bad spare parts situation. If it goes on like this I will soon be bankrupt. It is, however, said that resupply of spare parts is due at Tripoli.'

Turrets from captured Matilda tanks were emplaced by Italian troops near Halfaya Pass, in Egypt near the Libyan border, to bolster Axis defences.

Knocked-out British Mark VI (A15) Crusader tanks. The *Panzertruppenschule* II at Wünsdorf instructed in October 1941 that 'targets on British tanks are: the skirting, which buckles easily (protective covering); the stern; the driving sprocket; the tracks; and the lower corners of the turret.'

Max Reisch, former commander of a DAK vehicle maintenance unit, wrote of his attachment for a captured Jeep: 'The Volkswagen was underpowered and over open country it had to be driven mostly in low gear ... We called them *Flitzer* ['whizzer'] because you could whizz around in them absolutely anywhere.'

The NSU *Kleines Kettenkraftrad* HK 101, or Sd.Kfz. 2 *Kettenkrad*, was designed by NSU in 1939 as a light tractor. Although capable of negotiating steep slopes, care was needed driving this tall and a narrow vehicle. A total of 8,345 were produced during the war with another 550 assembled between 1946 and 1949.

Italian troops haul a *Cannone da* 47/32 M35. Built under license from the Austrian firm of Böhler, this lightweight weapon could fire both armour piercing and high explosive projectiles.

Former French *Canon de* 155 mm GPFT L/38 guns in German service were known as the 15.5cm K. 419 (f). With a range up to 21 kilometres, the crew of ten could fire two to three high explosive rounds per minute.

A captured Canadian Military Pattern (CMP) Chevrolet with a type 12 cab (known as the 'Alligator cab') 2-pounder portee. Such was Rommel's reliance on captured enemy transport that almost 80 per cent of the DAK's vehicle fleet was composed of enemy vehicles by the time of the Axis capitulation in May 1943.

Chevrolet CMP chassis with a Type 13 cab. German quartermasters could only dream of the standardisation of CMP vehicles in comparison to the miscellany of German types.

The Wünsdorf *Panzertruppenschule II* warned of British trucks that 'mount anti-tank guns on them with which they open fire unexpectedly over the stern or the engine. The British carry out dashing (reconnaissance) patrols by means of wheeled AFV's (armoured fighting vehicles) and on foot. They also appear from the desert to make thrusts deep into our rear lines, launching shock troops or attacking our rear columns with fast-wheeled armoured fighting vehicles.' The captured portee vehicles pictured mount 2-pounder (above) and 6-pounder (below) anti-tank guns.

Force landed Messerschmitt Bf 110 from *Zerstörergeschwader* 26, the first Luftwaffe formation sent to Africa.

One of a handful of Savoia-Marchetti SM.82s operated by *Stabsstaffel* /KG z.b.V. 1. The Luftwaffe acquired further examples after the Italian armistice.

Photographs from a Luftwaffe pilot's photo album showing Savoia-Marchetti SM.79 Sparviero bombers caught in a ghibli (left) and a Macchi C.202 *Folgore* (right).

North Africa was the proving ground for two Panzer *Selbstfahrlafette* II 7.5cm Kanone L/41 (Sf.) *auf Zugkraftwagen* 5t prototype halftracks at the beginning of 1942. Of the two, one was lost in action on 5 June after destroying three British tanks, the other captured by British forces.

Another rare vehicle was this field conversion of a Pz.Kpfw. III Ausf. H a 15cm sIG 33 L/11(Sf) *auf Fahrgestell Panzerkampfwagen* III Ausf. H (Sf). It is believed that this unique vehicle first saw action in September 1942.

Landwasserschlepper LWS 667 of *Pionier-Landungskompanie* 778. This rare amphibious tractor was to have participated in a landing behind enemy lines (with three captured Mk VI Cruiser 'Crusader' tanks) before the eventual cancellation of the operation on 29 May 1942.

According to a 1942 British combat report on the effectiveness of the 8.8cm Flak: 'The greatest single tank destroyer is the German 88-mm dual-purpose gun … on May 27th at 0800, Axis forces having enveloped Bir Hacheim, a German tank force of 60 tanks attacked the British 22nd Brigade some distance to the northeast. The British moved to attack this force with 50 light and medium American tanks. It soon became apparent that this British force was inadequate and the Brigadier commanding ordered a second regiment of 50 tanks into action. In 10 minutes the 88-mm German dual-purpose guns destroyed 8 American medium tanks of this reinforcing regiment. All day thereafter, the British engaged the enemy half-heartedly and finally withdrew. Sixteen American medium tanks were lost in all. These 16 fell victim, without a single exception, to the 88-mm dual-purpose gun.'

The Fall of Tobruk

Tobruk was attacked on the morning of 20 June 1942. Unlike the 242-day siege of the previous year, the fortress capitulated just 24 hours later.

Although Rommel later wrote that Tobruk was the windfall needed to keep his army marching on the Nile in terms of the 'vast booty that had fallen to us', the Germans, to their dismay, discovered that the port had an unexpectedly small unloading capacity, far from what was needed to ease their supply crisis.

Crossing the outer perimeter anti-tank ditch surrounding Tobruk. In actuality the ditch had silted up in many places and represented no obstacle to the attackers. The vehicle is a Ford type 01 Y with a South African-built body, a light truck from a medical company.

German columns approach Tobruk's harbour, the centre of the Allied bastion that had become an obsession for Rommel.

A Pz.Kpfw. III advances to within sight of the harbour. South-African born General Hendrik Klopper surrendered the ad hoc British garrison of 33,000 troops on the morning of 21 June 1942. Vast stores of arms, ammunition and clothing appropriated. One hundred tanks were captured, thirty of which were undamaged.

Jovial Italian troops celebrate the fall of Tobruk. In the wake of the victory, Second-lieutenant Federico Vallauri wrote to his mother that 'all we talk about here is Alexandria and Cairo, and having a dip in the Suez Canal – however dirty the water may be …'

Weary members of the DAK after the battle.

South African troops marching into captivity. Many South Africans manning the western perimeter never fired a shot before the surrender of the fortress was announced, a shock for many that led to recriminations against their senior officers in PoW camps.

Indian PoWs photographed on a captured truck outside the battered Roman Catholic church at Bardia.

Mersa Matruh fell to Rommel's thoroughly exhausted troops on 29 June 1942. The approaching truck is a Fiat 634.

Brigadier George Herbert Clifton, commander of the 6th New Zealand Brigade (far left), was captured by Italian paratroopers of the 187th *Reggimento Folgore* on 4 September 1942. Rommel often spoke with senior opponents taken prisoner. The health of the newly promoted German field marshal continued to deteriorate at this time, forcing him to return to Europe for a 'prolonged course of treatment'. His temporary replacement was General Georg Stumme, a veteran tank commander also in poor health and with no experience in desert warfare.

Wounded British tanks crews taken prisoner receive medical attention.

Life magazine noted in July 1942 that the 'master secret of war is to sock the enemy with more metal and explosive than he socks you with, at every point you meet him.' The Germans understood the fear generated by their 8.8cm gun on the battlefield and would fabricate dummy guns using telegraph poles while mobile weapons fired with deadly accuracy from adjacent positions. One account recorded how 'storms of 88-mm air burst swept over the battlefield,' indeed by one estimate 40 per cent of Australian casualities at El Alamein were caused by the fearsome 8.8cm gun.

The German Army, explained *Gefreiter* Werner Mork, took 'great care to establish official army brothels called euphemistically Army Care Stations (*Wehrmacht-Betreuungsstelle*). Even in Africa the army took care of their soldiers' needs – at least as far as sex was concerned – and in this way any sexual frustration could be relieved and eliminated. The use of these establishments was even open to our brothers in arms, the ladies coming from the land of our allies. The brothels were much appreciated and well used, the forward bordello at Matruh being not far behind the front line.' Mork found another 'establishment' at Tobruk; 'Although the place had been ravaged by the war, there was a bordello there that was very popular. Before we got there we heard stories about the army brothels, but nobody believed them, but once on the spot we could see for ourselves how well the army cared for its soldiers in Africa.'

Pushing ahead into Egypt, the laws of desert warfare began to work against Rommel – the further the advance the longer the supply lines; conversely as the British retreated the shorter their lines became. Insufficient capacity at Tobruk continued the reliance on Benghazi. The return trip for a supply column from Benghazi to the front took upwards of seven days. From Tripoli it took twice as long, regardless of driving twelve hours a day. Road convoys also faced the threat of aerial attacks, the RAF enjoying air superiority.

Drums of precious fuel for an army in desperate need. *Gefreiter* Werner Mork recalled how trucks 'maintained a respectful distance from each other so as not to present an easy target for enemy aircraft. The co-driver sat on the right-hand mudguard to keep a look out but also to watch the road for obstructions and potholes. It was also important not to lose sight of the vehicle ahead through the dust and sand that was thrown up.'

The Germans employed gliders to ferry men and *matériel* to North Africa as the toll on convoys crossing the Mediterranean escalated. First flown by famed aviatrix and test pilot Hanna Reitsch in 1937, the DFS (*Deutsches Forschungsinstitut für Segelflugzeug*) 230 could carry nine men.

The twin-boom Gotha Go 242 was designed to replace the DFS 230. First flown in 1941, *Gothaer Waggonfabrik* produced 1,528 of these heavy transport gliders between 1941 and 1943. Critically deficient in arms, ammunition and fuel, Rommel unsuccessfully asked for 196 anti-tank guns alone to be flown in by glider after the First Battle of Alamein. By late August 1942, German formations were short of some 15,000 men, 130 anti-tank guns and 210 tanks, 175 armoured cars and personnel carriers and 1,400 trucks.

El Alamein

Rommel's pursuit of the retreating Eighth Army ground to a halt on 3 July 1942, the DAK chronically short of supplies, his men exhausted with many ill from jaundice, gastro-enteritis and other desert maladies. Rommel too was ill, even requesting (unsuccessfully) for Berlin to replace him with General Heinz Guderian. Equipment-wise, his operational spearhead now numbered only fifty-five operational tanks, seventy-seven artillery pieces, and sixty-five anti-tank guns; the *Afrikakorps* comprised little more than 2,000 active combatants. As in the case of his first attacks at Tobruk in 1941, a comparable lack of reconnaissance stopped his frontal charge at the British El Alamein line, where it was only during battle that he discovered the depth of the enemy defences. Two attempts to drive through the newly established British front failed on 1 and 10 July. Rommel's subsequent failure at the Battle of Alam Haifa, between 13 August and 6 September, forced to him abandon mobile warfare and adopt a defensive position in depth. Meanwhile, the expanding British forces could concentrate on planning and training for an offensive breakthrough.

The terrain at El Alamein was quite unlike that traversed to date. Bordered by the Mediterranean to the north, Rommel faced another impassable sea 40 miles to the south – an impassable desert basin called the Qattara Depression. Caught in a geographical funnel, for the first time in the campaign Rommel was denied an open flank to route his opponent.

Troops of the Australian 9th Division – the Rats of Tobruk, refreshed after garrison duties in Syria – at the railway halt that was to mark the limit of Rommel's advance, El Alamein. Just sixty miles (95km) from Alexandria, it was here the decisive battle for Egypt was fought.

A soldier's snapshot of Churchill visiting the front at El Alamein on 5 August 1942. Churchill was instrumental in appointing Bernard Montgomery – Britain's first 'celebrity' general of the Second World War, as commander of the British 8th Army. Montgomery became the seventh British commander to face Rommel in the desert.

Warnings to the unwary of the proximity of German forces and the danger of minefields.

The Marder III, or *Panzerjäger* 38(t) für 7.62cm PaK36(r), served with the 15th Panzer Division (33rd *Panzerjäger Abteilung*) and 39th *Panzerjäger Abteilung*. An effective tank destroyer, it was armed with a captured Soviet 7.62cm anti-tank gun re-chambered to accept German 75mm Pak 40 ammunition. A total of 344 were built with sixty-six sent to North Africa.

Another German armoured amalgam to appear in the desert was the 15cm *schwerer Feldhaubitzer 13/1 (sfl) auf Geschützwagen Lorraine Schlepper (f)*, the mating of captured French Lorraine 37L tractors with a 15cm *schwerer Feldhaubitzer* 13 howitzer. Twenty-three of these self-propelled howitzers were landed at Tobruk and Benghasi. The first vehicles saw action on 30 August. All were reported lost by 2 December 1942. On 19 October *Panzerarmee Afrika* reported its strength as 234 German and 289 Italian tanks. Of the panzers, only 123 were up-to-date models including 88 Pz.Kpfw. IIIs with the long-barrelled 5.0cm gun and 35 Pz.Kpfw. IVs.

The M3 Grant (right) was a mainstay in the British 8th Army until the arrival of the M4 Sherman (left), which first saw combat at El Alamein. This versatile tank had thicker armour than the Cruiser tanks, was faster than the Infantry tanks and wielded a gun significantly better than the 2-pounder. Its success in the desert led to the Sherman becoming the backbone of the British tank force across Europe.

Rommel held senior deskbound officers in Berlin with contempt, believing in the maxim, '*Weit vom Schuss gibt alte Krieger*' ('Staying far from the battle makes for old soldiers'). Here he observes the fire from an ex-Soviet 76.2mm Model 1936 field gun converted for use as an anti-tank gun known as the 7.62cm PaK 36(r).

A camouflaged 15cm sFH18 heavy field howitzer. German artillery was taught to shoot first and correct afterwards. The shock of the first salvo, Rommel believed, was crucial in success on the battlefield.

Rommel pictured beside a captured 25-pounder, the standard British field gun of the Second World War. In the largest concentration of artillery since 1918, the British assembled 834 25-pounders and 48 medium guns in the opening barrage of the Second Battle of El Alamein on 23 October 1942. Over the following twelve days the 25-pounders fired over a million rounds – the equivalent of 102 rounds fired per gun each day.

Resting beside a 5.0cm *Panzerabwehrkanone* (Pak) 38 (L/60). A British report tabled in March 1942 on the destruction of forty-eight tanks during Operation Crusader (18 November – 30 December 1941) found that fourteen (29 per cent) were hit by 88mm rounds, seven (15 per cent) by 5.0cm rounds (either Pak 38 or Pz.Kpfw III), three (6 per cent) by 47mm rounds. The remaining twenty-four (50 per cent) succumbed to smaller caliber weapons, mines or mechanical breakdown.

Knocked-out Pz.Kpfw. IIIs litter the Western Desert battlefield, one apparently torn apart by internal explosions to prevent its capture and/or reuse. The pivotal battle for Egypt began on the night of 23 October with an artillery barrage reminiscent of the First World War. Stumme was at the front the next day to gain a clearer picture of the fighting when he suffered a fatal heart attack. Hitler directed that Rommel return to Africa at once. In a letter to his wife on 3 November, a glum 'Desert Fox' penned: 'The battle still rages with unspent fury. I can no longer, or scarcely any longer, believe in its successful outcome.' The following day only 36 panzers, out of the 249 at the beginning of the battle, were still running.

A Pz.Kpfw. IV Ausf. F2 literally blown apart.

On 20 October 1942, there were some 152,000 Axis troops in Egypt, comprising 62,000 Italians and 90,000 Germans. Of this number, approximately 60,000 were positioned at El Alamein to face an Allied force of 195,000. German casualties from the battle, based on Ultra intercepts, were estimated at 1,149 killed, 3,886 wounded and 8,050 men captured; Italian losses were 971 dead, 933 wounded and 15,552 men captured. The total number of Axis prisoners had climbed to 30,000 by 11 November.

Hans von Luck recalled recalled how Rommel 'spoke of the terrible scenes that were taking place on the coastal road. Pursued by British tanks and covered inescapably by carpets of bombs, vehicles were left standing in flames, while the men tried to save themselves on foot. Owing to these insurmountable obstacles, the supply trucks were hardly able to make progress.' Note the column of wrecked Lancia 3RO *Autocannone da* 90/53 self-propelled guns (above).

The slogging match that was the Second Battle of El Alamein lasted from 23 October 1942 to 5 November, by which time Rommel's forces were in full retreat. Tobruk was retaken on 13 November, and by 23 November Rommel was back at El Agheila. Earlier, on 8 November, Anglo-US forces had landed in Morocco and Algeria. The slow advance of the Allies eastward from Algeria, however, permitted a Tunisian bridgehead to be consolidated and extended to the west. Von Luck wrote that 'Rommel looked exhausted. His uniform was worn and dusty. The hard withdrawal actions, his deep disappointment, and his illness, not yet fully cured, had left their mark on him.'

Weihnachten (Christmas) in the desert. Von Luck recalled that 'Christmas 1942 arrived but we had no time to celebrate … deep in the desert, without a tree or a bush, and in the heat of the day, our thoughts turned to home, where our families were having to endure air raids and food rationing.'

Chapter 9
1943 – The End

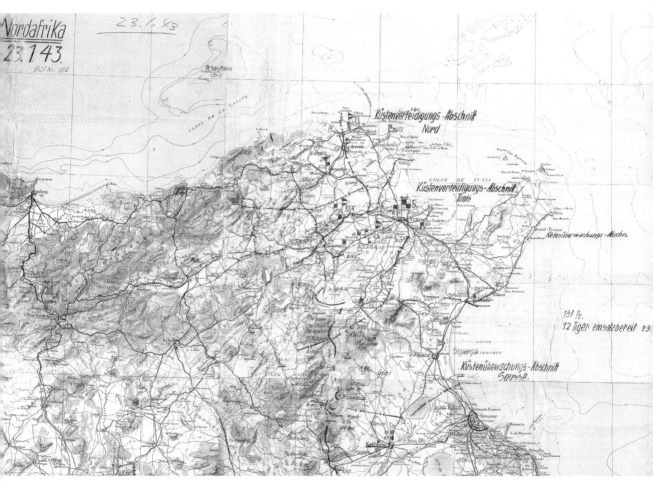

German situation map of Tunisia dated 23 January 1943, the day the British 8th Army finally entered the Libyan capital of Tripoli. Italy's African empire had collapsed. Sandwiched between the US-Anglo forces in French North Africa and Montgomery's advance from the east, the Axis rushed 250,000 German and Italian troops to Tunisia in a last-ditch effort to save their fading North African fortunes.

A warm welcome received from Tunisian Berbers;
the end of the Axis in North Africa imminent.

Max Reisch recalled 'in the few months left to us in Tunisia, we managed to strip this rich country of all
its produce. Rommel's emaciated soldiers poured in out of the desert like a swarm of locusts and fell upon
the fertile cultivations…At that time, when a lot of people were muttering the old 'Eat, drink and be merry'
proverb, we paraphrased it along the lines of, "Be merry in Tunis – at least you didn't die in Libya".'

German *Fallschirmjäger* (paratroops) were amongst the first Axis troops rushed to Vichy-held Tunisia.

German troops pictured at Mateur in northern Tunisia. Unlike the vast, open space of the Western Desert, the Tunisian topography offered ample opportunities to establish strong defences. Audacious 100 mile (160km) advances across open desert were now but a memory.

Newly arrived Pz.Kpfw. IIIs, possibly from the 10th Panzer Division. After action on the Eastern Front and a refit in France, the division was shipped to Tunisia in December 1942. It was destroyed in Tunis on 12 May 1943 and disbanded the following month.

The four-leaf clover on white square symbol identifies this Ford belonging to the Luftwaffe's 19th Flak Division. Formed in June-July 1942, it served under Rommel during the Tunisian campaign before surrendering in Tunis in May 1943. It was later reformed for the defence of Greece and Yugoslavia.

German and Italian troops examine an Italian 2mm *Cannone-Mitragliera da 20/65 modello 35* (Breda).

Exhausted and in poor physical health, Rommel left Tunisia on 9 March 1943, three days after his unsuccessful last offensive against the British at the Battle of Medenine. Succeeded by *Generaloberst* Hans-Jürgen von Arnim, the 'Desert Fox' never returned to North Africa. Meeting Mussolini in Rome, Rommel failed to persuade the Duce that a military withdrawal from Tunisia outweighed the political repercussions. A subsequent meeting with Hitler at his Ukrainian headquarters similarly failed to have his *Afrikaner* evacuated. Rommel spent several months on sick leave, followed by assignments in Greece (briefly) and Italy before a directive to oversee the Atlantic Wall.

Captured German anti-aircraft guns. From the left: 8.8cm-Flak 36; 8.8cm-Flak 41 (Note the long L/74 barrel); 8.8cm-Flak 41; 8.8cm-Flak 18; the remainder either Flak 18 or 36. The first batch of forty-four 8.8cm-Flak 41 guns were combat trialled in North Africa. Prone to jamming, only 556 were manufactured.

A US serviceman examines a captured 21cm *Nebelwerfer* 42. The shrieking sound made by the rockets leaving from the launcher unnerved many inexperienced US troops exposed to battle for the first time in Tunisia.

A 2cm *Flakvierling* 38 with a missing barrel. To the right is a 10.5cm leFH18 with wooden wheels.

The ignominy of defeat, German rifles piled high under the watchful eyes of Allied captors.

Captivity. *Generaloberst* Hans-Jürgen von Arnim photographed after the miscellany of Axis forces, including two Panzer Armies, surrendered on 13 May 1943. The defeat of nearly 250,000 German and Italian troops – dubbed 'Tunisgrad' – outstripped the capitulation of Field Marshal Friedrich Paulus' German Sixth Army three months earlier at Stalingrad. A total of 130,000 German and 180,000 Italians were taken prisoner. The Axis threat to the Middle East was removed. North Africa subsequently became the springboard for the subsequent Allied invasion of Sicily on 9 July. Draining more precious German resources from the Eastern Front, the invasion of Italy accelerated the fall of Mussolini (who was arrested on 25 July) and the demise of the Axis partnership.

Appendix: African Sketchbook

Nach dem
Angriff

Wilh.Wessel

Bildberichter Moosmüller
der PK-Afrika
22.4.1942
Will. Wessel

Bibliography

Official Records

Australian War Memorial (AWM), Canberra

AWM 3DRL 2632/37 Translation of Captured German documents

Britain

Report on Examination of German Light Aid Detachment Vehicle Type VW 82 'Volkswagen' produced by The Rootes Group, Engineering Dept., Humber Ltd., September 1943.

United States of America

US War Department, Military Intelligence Service. *German Methods of Warfare in the Libyan Desert.* Bulletin No. 20, July. Washington D.C., 1942.

———. *Artillery in the Desert. Special Series* No. 6, November 25. Washington D.C., 1942.

———. *The Libyan Campaign May 27 to July 27, 1942.* Campaign Study No. 4, January 18. Washington D.C., 1943.

Foreign Military Studies

Detwiler, *World War II German Military Studies,* Volume 7, Part IV, *The OKW War Diary Series, MS # C-065e.*

Detwiler, *World War II German Military Studies,* Volume 14, Part VI, *The Mediterranean Theatre, continued, MS# B-495.*

Historical Division European Command, Foreign Military Studies Branch. *German Experiences in Desert Warfare During World War II,* Vol. 1. MS # P-129.

Newell, C. R., *Egypt-Libya: The US Army Campaigns of World War II,* Defense Department, Army, Center of Military History 1993.

Supplement to Rommel's success, Reasons for, 1941-42. By Generalmajor Friedrich von Mellenthin MSS # D-024; D-084

Journal & Magazine Articles

Citino, R.M., Rommel in Africa, Drive to Nowhere. *MHQ Military History Quarterly 2012,* Summer 2012 Vol. 24, No. 4.

Katz, D., 'The Greatest Military Reversal of South African Arms: The Fall of Tobruk 1942, an Avoidable Blunder or an Evitable Disaster?' *Journal for Contemporary History* (2012).

Robinson, J.R., 'The Rommel Myth.' *Military Review* LXXVII, no. 5 (September-October 1997).

———. 'The Rommel Myth-Continued.' Letters to the Editor. *Military Review* LXXVIII (September-November 1998).

Westphal, S., 'Notes on the Campaign in North Africa.' *Journal of the Royal United Service Institution* 105 (February 1960).

Van Creveld, M., 'Rommel's Supply Problem, 1941-42.' *Journal of the Royal United Services Institute for Defence Studies* 119, No. 3 (September 1974).

Published Sources

Applegate, C. and P. Potter. *Music and German National Identity.* Chicago, 2002.

Bingham, J.K.W., and W. Haupt. *North African Campaign 1940-1943.* London, 1968.

Brinson, C. and R. Dove. *"Stimme Der Wahrheit": German-language Broadcasting by the BBC.* Amsterdam, 2003.

Burdick & Jacobson, *The Halder War Diary 1939-1942.* Novato [California], 1988.

Toppe, A., et al. *Desert Warfare: German Experiences in World War II,* reprint. Kansas 1991.

Behrendt, H-O. *Rommel's Intelligence in the Desert Campaign 1941-1943.* London, 1985.

Bender, J.R., and R.D. *Law, Uniforms, Organisation and History of the Afrikakorps*, San Jose [California], 1973.

Barker, A.J. *Afrika Korps*. London, 1978.

Barnett, C. *The Desert Generals*. New York, 1961.

Bungay, S. *Alamein*. London, 2003.

Citino, R.M. *Death of the Wehrmacht: The German Campaigns of 1942*. Lawrence [Kansas], 2011.

Edwards, R. *Scouts Out: A History of German Armored Reconnaissance Units in World War II*. Mechanicsburg [Pennsylvania], 2014.

Fennell, J. *Combat and Morale in the North African Campaign: The Eighth Army and the Path to El Alamein*. Cambridge, 2013.

Forty, G. *Afrika Korps at War Vol 1: The Road to Alexandria*. New York, 1978.

————. *Afrika Korps at War Vol 2: The Long Road Back*. New York, 1979.

Greene, J., and A. Massignani. *Rommel's North African Campaign, September 1940-November 1942*. Pennsylvania, 1994.

W. Gorlitz, ed., *The Memoirs of Field-Marshal Keitel: Chief of the German High Command, 1938-1945*.

Hartmann, B. *Panzers in the Sand, Vol Two: 1942-45: The History of Panzer-Regiment 5*. Mechanicsburg [Pennsylvania], 2011.

Heckman, W. *Rommel's War in Africa*. New York, 1981.

Hillenbrand F.K.M. *Underground Humour In Nazi Germany, 1933-1945*. Abingdon, 2014

Hinsley, F. H. *British Intelligence in the Second World War: Its influence on Strategy and Operations*, Volume I. London, 1979.

————. *British Intelligence in the Second World War: Its influence on Strategy and Operations*, Volume II. London, 1981

Hitler, A. *Hitler's Table Talk 1941-1944*. London, 1988.

Trevor-Roper, H.R., ed. *Hitler's War Directives 1939-1945*. London, 1964.

Irving, D. *The Trail of the Fox: The Life of Field-Marshal Erwin Rommel*. Hertfordshire, 1977.

Jentz, T. *Tank Combat in North Africa, The Opening Rounds, Operations Sonnenblume, Brevity, Skorpion and Battleaxe February 1941-June 1941*. Atglen [Pennsylvania], 1998.

Kesselring, A. *The Memoirs of Field-Marshal Kesselring*. London, 1974.

Liddell Hart, B.H., ed. *The Rommel Papers*. London, 1953.

Lewin, R. *Rommel as Military Commander*. New York, 1968.

————. *The Life and Death of the Afrika Korps*. London, 1977.

Marshall, C.F. *Discovering the Rommel Murder: The Life and Death of the Desert Fox*. London, 2002.

McQuirk, D. *Rommel's Army in Africa*. London, 1987.

————. *Afrikakorps: Self Portrait*. London, 1992.

Mitchelhill-Green, D. *Tobruk 1942*. Stroud [Gloucestershire], 2016

Nafziger, G.F., *The Afrika Korps: An Operational History 1941-1943*. West Chester [Ohio], 1997.

Piekalkiewicz, J. *Rommel and the Secret War in North Africa, 1941-1943*. West Chester, [Ohio] 1992.

Reisch, M. *Out of the Rat Trap: Desert Adventures with Rommel*. Stroud [Gloucestershire], 2013.

Schmidt, H.W. *With Rommel in the Desert*. London, 1951.

Schraepler, H.A. *At Rommel's Side: The Lost Letters of Han Joachim Schraepler*, London, 2009.

Schreiber, G. et al. *Germany and the Second World War, Volume III: The Mediterranean, South-east Europe, and North Africa 1939-1941*. Oxford, 1995.

Villahermosa, G. *Hitler's Paratrooper: The Life and Battles of Rudolf Witzig*. Barnsley, 2014.

Von Luck, H. *Panzer Commander*. New York, 1989.

Von Mellenthin, F. W. *Panzer Battles*. New York, 1956.

Weal, J., Junkers *Ju 87: Stukageschwader of North Africa and the Mediterranean*. London, 1998.

Westphal, S. *The German Army in the West*. London, 1951